Catholic Social Teaching: A New Synthesis

Rerum Novarum to *Laudato Si'*

By Daniel Schwindt

Follow the author at:
https://www.patreon.com/danielschwindt

Catholic Social Teaching: A New Synthesis
Copyright © 2015 Daniel Schwindt

ISBN-13: 978-0692470381
ISBN-10: 0692470387

To request permission to make copies of any part of this work, please contact:

Daniel Schwindt (Author/Editor)
McPherson, KS 67460
+1 620-755-8832
daniel.schwindt@gmail.com

If one member suffer anything, all the members suffer with it; or if one member glory, all the members rejoice with it.

~ 1 Corinthians 12:26

Woe to you that join house to house and lay field to field, even to the end of the place: shall you alone dwell in the midst of the earth?

~ Isaiah 5:8

The hireling flieth, because he is a hireling.

~ John 10:13

When the neighboring peoples bring merchandise or grain to sell on the Sabbath, we will not buy from them on the Sabbath or on any holy day. Every seventh year we will forgo working the land and will cancel all debts.

~ Nehemiah 10:31

Contents

Abbreviations

AA	*Apostolicam Actuositatem*
AM	*Apostolic Mandate*
CA	*Centesimus Annus*
CC	*Casti Connubii*
CCC	*Catechism of the Catholic Church*
CSDC	*Compendium of the Social Doctrine of the Church*
CV	*Caritas in Veritate*
DH	*Dignitatis Humanae*
DR	*De Regno*
DV	*Donum Vitae*
EG	*Evangelii Gaudium*
EN	*Evangelii Nuntiandi*
EV	*Evangelium Vitae*
FC	*Familiaris Consortio*
GS	*Gaudium et Spes*
HG	*Humanum Genus*
HV	*Humanae Vitae*
ID	*Immortale Dei*
LC	*Libertatis Conscientia*
LE	*Laborem Exercens*
LP	*Libertas Praestantissimum*
LS	*Laudato Si'*
MM	*Mater et Magistra*
OA	*Octogesima Adveniens*
PDG	*Pascendi Dominici Gregis*
PP	*Populorum Progressio*
PT	*Pacem in Terris*
QA	*Quadragesimo Anno*
RH	*Redemptor Hominis*
RN	*Rerum Novarum*
RP	*Reconciliatio et Paenitentia*
SRS	*Sollicitudo Rei Socialis*
ST	*Summa Theologica*
TFP	*Tametsi Futura Prospicientibus*

UA   *Ubi Arcano*
VS   *Veritatis Splendor*

Introduction

1. The purpose of this book

In the recently released *Laudato Si'*, Pope Francis issued the following challenge:

> "We need to develop a new synthesis capable of overcoming the false arguments of recent centuries. Christianity, in fidelity to its own identity and the rich deposit of truth which it has received from Jesus Christ, continues to reflect on these issues in fruitful dialogue with changing historical situations. In doing so, it reveals its eternal newness."[1]

This book represents one attempt by a member of the laity to meet that challenge. That being the justification for the existence of such a work as this, it is also necessary to state clearly the approach we will take in the pages that follow, because it may differ substantially from that to which the reader is accustomed. In order to accomplish this, we may simply borrow the words of Harold Robbins, who opened his most excellent book, *The Sun of Justice*, by saying:

> "This book is not an analysis of what the Church tolerates, and in tolerating guides. It seeks to be a statement of what the Church wants...The distinction, which seems self-evident, is made surprisingly seldom. The Church has her negative standards, to fall below which is to fall into sin. These standards are necessarily minimum standards, for Moral Theology is conditioned by Charity. But she has also her positive standards, which are very different. I am informed by my clerical friends that the only name for these is Ascetic Theology. It seems strange to me that to want to do what the Church approves should be a striving after Asceticism, at least in its ordinary sense. Please God the desire is more general than that

---

[1] *LS*, 121.

would imply. But we need not discuss this further. The point is that our outlook on society has been too much in terms of the confessional, and too little in terms of the City of God. A man could avoid the sin of being theologically drunk every night of his life, and give a very poor impression to his neighbours of the Virtue of Temperance. And millionaires are not excommunicated for being millionaires, but no one who is familiar with the blistering phrases of Popes Leo XIII and Pius XI can suppose that they are at all pleased that millionaires should exist. I see no reason why the laity should be pleased, either."[2]

That having been said, we can add that our work here will hopefully serve to dispel the fog of ignorance that has settled on the faithful in our period; an ignorance which, although understandable for men and women who must work for their bread, and who therefore do not have the time, energy, or desire to thumb through hundreds of years of papal statements, is nonetheless very dangerous. We no longer live in the age of obedience when the unlearned would turn with childlike openness to the Church, ready to trust Rome's counsel. On the contrary, in democratic ages every man is told to "think for himself." He is led to believe that the opinions he arrives at by the power of his own judgment are the supreme measure of truth in his world, with the end result that his opinions are formed almost entirely by voices emitting from his television set. For there is no such thing as an opinion formed "independently." We are all of us under the influence of a million pressures external to ourselves; it is only a matter of which of those influences we allow to guide our reasoning.

And so, in this "age of information," every man in America knows about the latest earthquake in the third-world, able to cite the "death toll" down to the last woman and child; he knows about the most recent mass-shooting or terrorist plot; he knows which celebrities are getting divorced: but this same man has no idea whatsoever of the Catholic doctrines related to subsidiarity, solidarity, the universal destination of

---

[2] Harold Robbins, *Sun of Justice* (London, 1938), p. 9.

goods, and private property. Even if he has heard of them, they have been filtered through the political medium, which is to say they have been mutilated beyond recognition. Not for a thousand dollars could he name the magnificent documents in which these principles are elaborated, even though they are every one of them at his fingertips, thanks to the internet.

Thus, we find that although we have more information at our disposal than during any previous period, it seems that the truths of Catholic Social Teaching have been enveloped by an ocean of talk shows, radio broadcasts, and webpages, leaving us in the dark to stumble haphazardly through every problem that arises. In this situation, we cannot help but recall the lamentation of Pius X, which applies to our time much more than it did his:

> "[T]he will cannot be upright nor the conduct good when the mind is shrouded in the darkness of crass ignorance. A man who walks with open eyes may, indeed, turn aside from the right path, but a blind man is in much more imminent danger of wandering away...How many and how grave are the consequences of ignorance in matters of religion!...It is indeed vain to expect a fulfillment of the duties of a Christian by one who does not even know them."[3]

The larger purpose of this book, then, is to inject the truths of the Christian tradition into the ocean of incoherence in which the modern man is forced to live—to beat back the waters of confusion and ignorance, even if only a little, and give him the opportunity to breath the clean air of Catholic doctrine.

We might also mention that this book was produced almost by accident while collecting notes for a very different project of a more ambitious nature. At one point, after arranging copious notes for that separate project, we realized that, due to the concise nature and arrangement of

---

[3] *AN*, 5-6.

those subjects and citations, the information which we had collected might serve as a useful tool for others whose interest in Catholic Social Teaching coincides with our own.

Anyone who makes the claim that "the Church teaches such-and-such" ought to be ready immediately to produce the appropriate documentation as support for their assertion. Therefore, we will attempt to provide a handful of references for each subject we address. The task has not been difficult, thanks to the constant labor of the Church through the centuries to address problems as they arise. Indeed, we can rest confident that there are few social questions that the Church has not wrestled with in her history. Because of this diligence, any claims as to her opinion one way or the other on some specific issue are almost always readily verifiable. The explanation for the various debates that persist on so many issues is not, we must admit, due to silence on the part of the Church, but rather ignorance on the part of the public. There was perhaps a time when it was legitimate to blame the Church for the ignorance of her people, but today there is simply no excuse for it. The Vatican has taken steps to make thousands of its texts readily available online, including the excellent *Compendium of the Social Doctrine of the Church*. Truthfully, while we could mention a few valid disagreements about the nature of Church teaching, the vast majority of such disputes could be dispelled in a moment if the participants would simply pause to reference their sources. It is our hope that the present work may encourage and facilitate this process.

2. Toward the Jubilee

In order to wrap our minds around the subject we have before us, we can begin by referring to an Old Testament custom known as the Jubilee. A brief review of this tradition is helpful because the Jubilee has been described by the Church as an illustration of *Catholic Social Doctrine in miniature*.[4] It can therefore be seen as an incredibly compact summary of the teachings we are about to explore.

---

[4] *CSDC*, 25; *LS*, 71.

Catholic Social Teaching (hereafter "CST") has for its goal the stability and justice of social life. This means that it is relevant in some way to any society at any time. Most of us tend to imagine CST as a body of Church documents written to combat the evils of the modern industrial period. That is to say, we unconsciously attribute to CST a purely "reactionary" character—something necessitated by extreme circumstances but otherwise irrelevant. But obviously any doctrine that is *only* reactionary is not a doctrine, because doctrines are timeless, placeless, and purely affirmative. They are *positive*. If any doctrine seems like a reaction to a specific historical period, it can only be because that period chose to deny it. And so, if the principles enunciated in *Rerum Novarum* seem to be a reaction to socialism or capitalism, this is only because those two ideologies tried very hard to ignore them, and because they insisted on ignoring them, Pope Leo XIII had to re-affirm them. He said nothing new.

We may pause and make sure we are justified in what we've claimed, which is that the social teachings of the Church are not modern, born of the Industrial Revolution, but timeless. If we are going to say that the social teachings of the Church go back further than *Rerum Novarum*, capitalism, and socialism, then we had better be able to explain where exactly they do go back to. This leads us to refer to one of the oldest records we have—the Old Testament—where God Himself directly specifies the economic institutions of His people. One such institution is the Year of Jubilee. Quoting the *Compendium of the Social Doctrine of the Church*:

> "Among the many norms which tend to give concrete expression to the style of gratuitousness and sharing in justice which God inspires, the law of the sabbatical year (celebrated every seven years) and that of the jubilee year (celebrated every fifty years) stand out as important guidelines...The precepts of the sabbatical and jubilee years constitute a kind of social doctrine in miniature."[5]

---

[5] *CSDC*, 24, 25.

For agreement on this point, the writers of the *Compendium* turn to St. John Paul II, who said that "The social doctrine of the Church, which has always been a part of Church teaching and which has developed greatly in the last century, particularly after the Encyclical *Rerum Novarum*, is rooted in the tradition of the jubilee year."[6]

Clearly, then, when Leo XIII titled his document "On New Things," the *things* he had in mind were not the principles he was teaching, but the problems he was solving, problems that would not have arisen if the "Old Things" had not been forgotten.

But if the Jubilee is really the "root" of CST, and if it really does represent this doctrine "in miniature," then we ought to be able to derive the principles of CST from the Old Testament institution. Therefore, in order to justify the *Compendium*, let us take the central principles of CST as they are commonly given, namely: solidarity, subsidiarity, justice, the just price, the universal destination of goods, private property, and the preferential option for the poor. Following Pope Francis, we will also examine how the Jubilee expresses respect for creation, showing an explicit concern for the welfare of the land. Let us see how these truths find concise expression in the Old Testament institution.

To get a proper start, we will cite the scriptural outline of the Jubilee as found in the book of Leviticus. The basic principle is *cyclical*, reflecting the rhythms of human life and nature itself. It revolves around periods of rest (given to the land every seven years) and redemption (a large-scale economic reset every fifty years):

> "Six years thou shalt sow thy field and six years thou shalt prune thy vineyard, and shalt gather the fruits thereof: But in the seventh year there shall be a sabbath to the land, of the resting of the Lord: thou shalt not sow thy field, nor prune thy vineyard."[7]

---

[6] *TMA*, 13.

[7] *Lev* 25:3-6

"Thou shalt also number to thee seven weeks of years, that is to say, seven times seven, which together make forty-nine years…And thou shalt sanctify the fiftieth year, and shalt proclaim remission to all the inhabitants of thy land: for it is the year of jubilee. Every man shall return to his possession, and every one shall go back to his former family."[8]

"In the year of the jubilee all shall return to their possessions."[9]

The passage continues on at some length, but what can we say of it so far?

i. Solidarity

First, we see the undeniable expression of *solidarity*. St. Paul said that we were all one body, and that "if one member suffer anything, all the members suffer with it; or if one member glory, all the members rejoice with it."[10] While it is common today to applaud this notion *in theory*, implementing a sentimental but not a practical solidarity, it is another thing entirely to build it into the economic structure of society. Such was the purpose of the Jubilee:

"The jubilee year was meant to restore equality among all the children of Israel, offering new possibilities to families which had lost their property and even their personal freedom. On the other hand, the jubilee year was a reminder to the rich that a time would come when their Israelite slaves would once again become their equals and would be able to reclaim their rights."[11]

ii. Subsidiarity

But at the very same time we see the implementation of the other side of the solidarity coin, which is *subsidiarity*. Consider the fact that in

---

[8] *Lev* 25:8-10
[9] *Lev* 25:13
[10] Cf. *1 Cor* 12:12-26.
[11] *TMA*, 13.

this system economic activity is left to run its course 49 years out of 50. A less obtrusive government policy is indeed hard to imagine. But since the values agreed upon in private exchanges are, like man himself, bound to be imperfect, it is necessary for the political authority to intervene periodically in order to restore harmonious cooperation amongst participants.

iii. Justice

And so we move to a third principle, which is the harmonious relationship between *commutative* and *distributive* justice, taught by St. Thomas Aquinas and affirmed by the Church. In the Jubilee framework, individuals are allowed to carry out (provided they do not commit usury and other forms of theft) their day-to-day commerce as they see fit. Yet due to the imperfection of these transactions, errors accumulate in the system, contributing to an ever-increasing economic disharmony. The distribution of wealth inevitably begins to reflect this disharmony, which is to say the system becomes imbalanced. The political authority must then intervene to correct the accumulation of errors by wiping the slate clean, superimposing distributive justice on top of the framework of commutative justice, thereby balancing the scale and completing one "revolution" of the cycle. By incorporating such "intentional revolutions" into economic life, the "unintentional revolutions"— uncontrolled, unjust, and almost always violent—are defused before they begin.

iv. The Just Price

But by what measure are we to judge the justice or injustice of private exchanges in any scheme?—those through which so many small disharmonies are introduced into the overall system? The answer comes in the passage immediately following the one cited above:

> "When thou shalt sell any thing to thy neighbour, or shalt buy of him; grieve not thy brother: but thou shalt buy of him according to the number of years from the jubilee. And he shall sell to thee according to the computation of the fruits. The more years remain after the jubilee, the more shall the price increase: and the less time

is counted, so much the less shall the purchase cost. For he shall sell to thee the time of the fruits."[12]

Here we find an objective criterion for pricing which results from and presupposes the cyclical aspect of the Jubilee economy. Because land purchased immediately after the Jubilee may potentially have 49 years to produce, the one who acquires it will rightly pay a high price, and this price corresponds to the "computation of the fruits," which is to say, the produce which the land will yield and which will multiply with each year. Moreover, and for obvious reasons, land acquired a year before Jubilee will cost far less, because the produce of one season is all that will be factored into its price.

v. Private Property and the Universal Destination of Goods

We can see from the above that the legislation in Leviticus, like the tradition of the Church, affirms the institution of private property, but at the same time, also like the Church, takes care to subordinate private property to the original purpose of creation *as a gift to all of mankind*. It is within this universal context that the land is bought and sold, and it is for this reason that it cannot be sold permanently:

> "The land also shall not be sold for ever: because it is mine, and you are strangers and sojourners with me. For which cause all the country of your possession shall be under the condition of redemption."[13]

St. John Paul II elaborates on this principle:

> "It was a common conviction, in fact, that *to God alone, as Creator, belonged the 'dominium altum'*—lordship over all Creation and over the earth in particular (cf. *Lev* 25:23). If in his Providence God had given the earth to humanity, that meant that he had given it to everyone. Therefore *the riches of Creation were to be considered as a common good of the whole of humanity*. Those who possessed

---

[12] *Lev* 25:14-17
[13] *Lev* 25:23-24

these goods as personal property were really only stewards, ministers charged with working in the name of God, who remains the sole owner in the full sense, since it is God's will that created goods should serve everyone in a just way. *The jubilee year was meant to restore this social justice.*"14

vi. Widely Distributed Ownership

Reconciling itself to this theology of property, the Hebrew law ensured that anyone who had been forced through hardship to sell his land to another would be allowed to "redeem" it or buy it back at a later date. The price he must pay would again be computed through the Jubilee-style prorate system.

It is worth pausing to consider the implications of this prorate: if a man lost his land, he could at least rest assured that he had lost it when its price was *high*. He would know that every year following the loss, its redemption price would decrease, becoming more within his reach. As a consequence, the price for land would be at its *lowest* toward the end of the Jubilee cycle, even though this is the point at which concentration, and with it demand, would have normally reached its highest. Land speculation in this system is virtually impossible, or if it occurs it is at least not profitable; and this is so not merely because of the Jubilee, but because of the prorate scheme that is made possible by it, which corresponds to the just price and encourages a widely diffused pattern of ownership.

vii. Preferential Option for the Poor

Continuing through the passage:

> "If thy brother be impoverished, and weak of hand, and thou receive him as a stranger and sojourner, and he live with thee, Take not usury of him nor more than thou gavest: fear thy God, that thy brother may live with thee. Thou shalt not give him thy money upon usury, nor exact of him any increase of fruits."15

---

14 *TMA*, 13.

Obviously the intention here is to prohibit usury and prevent the growth of debt-slavery, but the underlying spirit, if we consider the Jubilee doctrine as a whole, is a concern for the poor. Every limit and mechanism it implements confirms this intention. Thus, we can see again why St. John Paul II said that:

> "Justice, according to the Law of Israel, consisted above all in the protection of the weak, and a king was supposed to be outstanding in this regard, as the Psalmist says: 'He delivers the needy when he calls, the poor and him who has no helper. He has pity on the weak and the needy, and saves the lives of the needy' (*Ps* 72:12-13)."[16]

vii. Concern for Creation

Especially in light of *Laudato Si'*, it is vital to recall the passage quoted at the beginning:

> "Six years thou shalt sow thy field and six years thou shalt prune thy vineyard, and shalt gather the fruits thereof: But in the seventh year there shall be a sabbath to the land, of the resting of the Lord: thou shalt not sow thy field, nor prune thy vineyard."[17]

Here the Sabbath is granted *to the land*, which is to say, it is not only a symbolic rest, representative of spiritual rest and nothing else, but rather it has a very real material function. It is both meaningful *and necessary*. Anyone remotely familiar with agricultural technique can understand why this is so, and what negative results come about if the land is worked ceaselessly, without variety, and without opportunity to replenish itself. It will become sterile, devoid of that natural vigor which only periodic rest can maintain.

vii. Conclusion

---

15 *Lev* 25:35-37
16 *TMA*, 13.
17 *Lev* 25:3-6

The ultimate value of the Jubilee is to remind us that all of our social arrangements—money, property, markets—are human things. They are devised and executed through human reasoning, a noble but imperfect faculty, with the intention of imitating Divine Justice. All of our systems will inevitably fall short, accumulate errors, and crash. And this remains true whether the crash is immediate and obvious and leads to a great depression, or whether it is monotonous, laborious, and even perpetual.

The doctrine of the Jubilee serves the twofold purpose of being a reminder in spiritual affairs and providing a reset in material affairs. We need the reminder because we are human, and we forget that our justice is not the ultimate justice.

3. Remarks on Sources Used

We have chosen to dwell at length on the Jubilee because, not only does it serve as a useful illustration of CST, but at the same time it reveals the timelessness of Catholic principles. Having established this basis, we will begin to make extensive use of those documents which are much more recent. In addition to the use of scripture, the Church Fathers, and various official documents produced by the Church itself, we will make frequent use of the Angelic Doctor, St. Thomas Aquinas. We feel comfortable utilizing an individual such as Aquinas only because, in doing so, we are conforming to the attitude of the popes themselves. St. Pius X was not expressing a private opinion when he said:

> "In the first place, with regard to studies, We will and ordain that scholastic philosophy be made the basis of the sacred sciences...And let it be clearly understood above all things that the scholastic philosophy We prescribe is that which the Angelic Doctor has bequeathed to us...Further, let Professors remember that they cannot set St. Thomas aside, especially in metaphysical questions, without grave detriment."[18]

---

[18] *PDG*, 45.

We will also attempt to limit our study specifically to those sources which are readily available on the internet. Every source used here, from the *Compendium of the Social Doctrine of the Church,* to the *Catechism*, to the *Summa Theologica* of St. Thomas Aquinas, can be found online by anyone with an internet connection. My hope is that most readers will take advantage of this fact in order to verify and study in greater depth any sources they find meaningful or interesting.

The various encyclicals, the *Compendium*, the *Catechism*, and most of the other documents cited below are available at the Vatican website: http://www.vatican.va/archive/index.htm

The *Summa Theologica* of St. Thomas Aquinas, *The Catholic Encyclopedia* and many other significant writings are available from New Advent: www.newadvent.org

The remainder of Aquinas' works can be obtained from the *Dominican House of Studies*: www.dhspriory/thomas

Finally, the reader should be aware that we will not limit ourselves only to those documents normally associated with CST—which is in fact a very specific and limited corpus. This is because the documents specifically associated with CST, in their approach and in their manner of speaking, often take for granted a certain degree of familiarity with doctrine. This is a degree of familiarity which, in our time, it is not possible to presume.

For example, all of the documents of CST presuppose an acceptance of Catholic moral philosophy, which, sadly, is often lacking. Even those members of the laity who are open to the teachings, and who believe themselves to be in complete conformity with the Magisterial position, may find that in fact they have never even heard of some of her principles. And so, when we arrive in our study at sections which presuppose Catholic moral philosophy, we will veer away from the corpus of CST in order to explore documents from other areas, such as St. John Paul II's moral encyclical, *Veritatis Splendor*. This is not because *Veritatis Splendor* is the only document to speak on morality, but because it is the first document to synthesize the moral teachings of the Church for the benefit of all its members and to publish them in such succinct form. As the document itself states:

> "This is the first time…that the Magisterium of the Church has set forth in detail the fundamental elements of this teaching, and presented the principles for the pastoral discernment necessary in practical and cultural situations which are complex and even crucial."[19]

Other "necessary digressions" of this sort may be expected to occur throughout the work.

---

[19] *VS*, 115.

Section I. The Role of the Church

1. Justification for the doctrine

At one time it would have been taken for granted that the Church—whose business is to guide and form the profound aspects of man's being—would also have something to say about his mundane economic activities. Unfortunately, this is no longer the case. Men today are trained to imagine various compartments in life: one "personal" and one "spiritual," one "recreational" and one "professional," one "public" and one "private." As a result the Church and the State, and even more so the Church and "the market," are cordoned off and told they have nothing to say about one another. Thus, we find ourselves reduced to a position from which we must justify the very existence of the doctrines we are about to explore. Before we can say what the Church teaches about economic and political life, we must convince the reader of Church's right to have any opinion whatsoever in these matters. Fortunately the task is not difficult.

a. Grace presupposes nature

If it be asked why the Church should concern itself with "worldly affairs" and issues seemingly so far-removed from religion as economic theory, we can respond plainly that these two spheres are not really as distant from one another as the materialists and technocrats would have us believe. Yet a more comprehensive explanation is called for if we are to understand not only why the Church is justified in formulating this doctrine, but also why, once formulated, *it deserves to be obeyed*.

We may find such a justification by referring to the maxim of St. Thomas Aquinas, that *grace presupposes nature*.[20]

That is to say, the spiritual dimension of man's being, in which his true happiness is to be found and which is the supreme concern of the

---

[20] *ST* I-II, q. 2, a. 1.

Church, is not to be imagined as existing in some other world, sharply divided from the "ordinary" world in which we live out our daily lives. The Christian tradition does not buy into such a dichotomy. It teaches that man is neither material body nor incorporeal soul, but is rather a *union* of body-and-soul. *Grace*, then, or the life of the spirit, presupposes and is built upon the foundation of *nature*. And while it is true that the foundation is hierarchically inferior to the superstructure (grace), it is still the foundation, and foundations are something of a necessity to the structures that rely them. Taking this premise into account, the suggestion that spiritual authorities should not concern themselves with economic and political affairs and instead "stick to religion" is evidence that the speaker has made one of two great errors.

First, it is possible that he imagines that the higher order of reality (spiritual life) has nothing to do with the lower order (the physical world). From such a point of view, it is possible to conceive of a Church whose "sphere of competence" is religion alone, and whose business therefore has nothing to do with earthly life. This is probably the more common mistake. It is closely connected with the modern tendency already mentioned above, to try and organize ("systematize") life into neatly divided categories. Unfortunately, given such a view of life, and because physical realities press themselves upon our senses incessantly, sooner or later the material concerns begin to claim most, if not all, of one's attention. By going down this road, a man begins by dividing two orders of reality into separate worlds, and he ends by losing one of those worlds entirely as it fades from his consciousness. His point of view becomes an implicit, and sometimes also and explicit, materialism.

If we avoid the first mistake and manage to retain both orders of reality in our considerations, we must also guard against a second error, which comes from a misunderstanding of the hierarchical relationship between the spiritual and the material orders. In this case, even though the spiritual order is not lost, it is still hopelessly alienated from "worldly affairs" due to imagining the two orders as being "separate but equal," when in fact they can only be comprehended hierarchically.

To understand the nature of this second error, consider two strangers who meet on the street. They are distinct and roughly equal—and for this reason it is improper for one to interfere with the business of the other. This is an appropriate view of two men on the street, but it is not an appropriate view of the relationship between the Church and the State, because this latter is one of hierarchy and not of equality. This type of relationship can be illustrated interpersonally by imagining a father and child. The father can and should interfere in the life of the child. And from the point of view of the child, the reverse is true: he cannot command the father, but instead should listen to what the father commands because he is by nature in a subordinate position.

Such is the nature of all hierarchical relationships. While the inferior cannot comprehend or inform the superior, the superior can always comprehend and *should inform* the inferior. And so, while the lower cannot transgress into the higher, the higher is in a legitimate position to guide the lower. Traditionally speaking, this is the proper view of the relationship between the Church and authorities of a strictly worldly order.

b. The "soul" of the social body

We must be careful here. Although we have said that the spiritual authority is the superior and that it may speak into the inferior, we must also be clear that it only speaks to the affairs of the inferior regarding universal principles, since these are its area of expertise. It does not, as we shall note below, provide "technical solutions" to economic or political problems, for these technical and "practical" solutions are the proper domain of political authorities. It is precisely at this point that the Church acknowledges their autonomy. This hierarchical relationship, which carefully combines desire for unity with respect for autonomy, has been called the "Gelasian diarchy," named after a letter from Pope Gelasius I to Emperor Anastasius in the year 494 AD, when the pope advised the emperor as follows:

> "There are two powers, august Emperor, by which this world is chiefly ruled, namely, the sacred authority of the priests and the

royal power. Of these that of the priests is the more weighty, since they have to render an account for even the kings of men in the divine judgment."[21]

Pope Leo XIII affirmed this tradition when he said that "the Almighty...has given the charge of the human race to two powers, the ecclesiastical and the civil, the one being set over divine, and the other over human, things," but he also made sure to note that there must "exist between these two powers a certain orderly connection which may be compared to the union of the soul and body in man."[22] No one familiar with the connection between body and soul would suggest that the soul should disregard the activity and function of the body.

c. Faith and morals

Many of the Church's critics tend to parrot tirelessly certain phrases whenever a pope speaks about economic or political problems. They say that the Church's competence lies in "faith and morals," the obvious implication being that socio-economic issues are excluded from these two categories. Unfortunately, this is not the traditional understanding of social, economic, and political life. Morality, in fact, pervades all of these areas. Justice is the foundation of morality, and it is undeniable that economic affairs in particular are riddled with problems of justice. If these problems are left unanswered, they may result in chaos. This is why canon law claims:

> "To the Church belongs the right always and everywhere to announce moral principles, including those pertaining to the social order, and to make judgments on any human affairs to the extent that they are required by the fundamental rights of the human person or the salvation of souls."[23]

---

[21] Trans. John S. Ott, Portland State University, from Andreas Thiel, ed., *Epistolae Romanorum pontificum genuinae et quae ad eos scriptae sunt a S. Hilaro usque ad Pelagium II.*, vol. 1 (Brunsberg: Eduard Peter, 1867), Letter no. 12, pp. 349-358.

[22] *ID*, 14.

d. When the worldly undermines the eternal

Returning to our principle that *grace presupposes nature*, we can say that the Church has concern for the worldly, not because she wishes to dictate the details of its technical operations, but because man needs a healthy material foundation if his spiritual life is to thrive to its utmost. The Church concerns itself with temporal affairs only insofar as they threaten spiritual affairs, which means that her concern will necessarily expand in times of turmoil and economic confusion. Particularly when the conditions of man's earthly existence drop below a certain minimum, the Church cannot and will not remain silent. It was precisely this situation which gave birth to, and fuels, the further development of CST:

> "…it is not rash by any means to say that the whole scheme of social and economic life is now such as to put in the way of vast numbers of mankind most serious obstacles which prevent them from caring for the one thing necessary; namely, their eternal salvation."[24]

Woe to the man who claims that economic and political conditions have no bearing on the spiritual life. Clearly it is due precisely to the Church's eternal concerns that she refuses to remain indifferent to temporal ones.[25]

2. Interpreting the signs of the times

We have already said that the Church acts as guardian of *universal truth*, and is not concerned with technical solutions.[26] She operates on certain permanent principles which, although they never change, may require new adaptations depending on the time and place in which they are to be applied. This is not because the truth is somehow "relative," or changing, but because man and his environment are constantly

---

[23] *Code of Canon Law*, canon 747, § 2.

[24] *QA*, 130.

[25] *CSDC*, 71; *EN*, 34.

[26] *LS*, 188.

changing. Each age brings its own peculiarities and its own problems. As an expert in humanity,[27] the Church's duty is to constantly observe the flux of social conditions, appraising these adjustments as to whether they are good or bad, and responding to them in language intelligible to each new generation.[28]

3. Continuity and renewal

The Church is tasked both with protecting the eternal and unchanging teachings of the Church, and with providing appropriate adaptations, interpretations, and, when necessary, re-interpretations, for each historical period. The Church must "become all things to all people,"[29] and while this does not in any way imply "compromise," it does mean that when a new epoch presents itself, altering the customs, language, and thought of a people, it is up to the Church to make sure that the Tradition, in its fullness, is presented in a way that is intact and yet comprehensible to them. On this point, the desire expressed by St. John Paul II is the perennial desire of the Church:

> "I wish principally…to reaffirm the continuity of the social doctrine as well as its constant renewal. In effect, continuity and renewal are a proof of the perennial value of the teaching of the Church…This twofold dimension is typical of her teaching in the social sphere. On the one hand it is constant, for it remains identical in its fundamental inspiration, in its 'principles of reflection,' in its 'criteria of judgment,' in its basic 'directives for action,' and above all in its vital link with the Gospel of the Lord. On the other hand, it is ever new, because it is subject to the necessary and opportune adaptations suggested by the changes in historical conditions and by the unceasing flow of the events which are the setting of the life of people and society."[30]

---

[27] *CSDC*, 61; *PP*, 13.
[28] *GS*, 4.
[29] *1 Cor* 9:19-23.
[30] *SRS*, 3; Cf. *OA*, 4.

4. Remarks on Vatican II

If we are going to take the Church seriously as an authority (and if we are not, then we are certainly wasting our time), then we must take the *whole* Church and not pick and choose certain parts as it pleases us. Now this seems easy in principle—but what happens when we come up against an apparent contradiction in the tradition itself? What happens if the Church seems to "change its mind" or becomes "a house divided against itself?"[31] Does this not force us to choose between one part of the church against another, whether we have in mind sects or historical periods? Such a situation is difficult, but it is the position of this book that no such contradictions exist in actuality, allowing the reader to rest knowing that he is not faced with a conundrum of this magnitude.

Controversy has arisen in the history of the Church—we should not be surprised at this, for it is said that *scandal must come*[32]—and these controversies demand explanation, especially since certain groups have used these moments of discord to divide the flock. The most recent controversy of this type is the debate surrounding the Second Vatican Council ("Vatican II"). Because of this controversy, any study of CST that tries to ignore the disagreements which followed Vatican II will doom its readers to confusion and frustration. We would not wish this trouble upon our readers, and so we will reconcile this debate without pausing on it any longer than is necessary. We will show that the division in question is only apparent, that the Tradition of the Church remains intact, and that the reader need not choose between the Church of Yesterday and the Church of Tomorrow, but can be at peace within the Church Eternal.

Admittedly the debates surrounding the Second Vatican Council have been the greatest threat to Catholic unity in the last century. Those who participate in the battle tend to take one of two positions which are, in our opinion, equally superficial: either Vatican II was an illegitimate compromise with the modernist heresy, and therefore all post-conciliar

---

[31] *Mt* 12:25
[32] *Mt* 18:7.

popes are "pretenders" and heretics themselves[33]; or else the Council represents a "coming around" of the Church to modern ways, which it had until then been obstinately and wrongly opposed.

Both of these views share one thing, and that is a pessimistic attitude toward the Church as a competent authority. *Both believe that Vatican II represents a departure from and a rejection of the previous teachings of the Church. They only differ on whether or not the change was good or bad.*

Moreover, both positions foster division. The first view requires the believer to stand against the Church as he finds it today, while the second requires the believer to stand against the Church as it was for a thousand years prior. This is why, although we may find respectable persons on either side of this debate, we ought to have no respect at all for the debate itself. In what follows, we will attempt to guide the reader around this tangled mess so that he can avoid such an unnecessary snare.

5. The example of Dignitatis Humanae

When it comes to such convoluted disputes, it is helpful to isolate a single element in the controversy which epitomizes it; and then, by dissecting this error, we are able to reach an understanding of the nature of the problem in its entirety.

In my experience, the most debated item from the council is its Declaration on religious freedom, *Dignitatis Humanae* (Latin: "Of the Dignity of the Human Person"). Compared to the controversy it has sparked, it is a remarkably short document, as well as very limited in its scope (which should automatically suggest to us that it ought to be read in a certain way). The source of the contention hinges on whether or

---

[33] This is the position of the "sedevacantists," whose name derives from the Latin *sede vacante* which means "the seat is vacant." The sedevacantists usually insist that the last legitimate pope was Pius XII, and that the seat has been vacant since his death in 1958.

not it overturns the previous teachings on religious worship and, in particular, the relationship of the State with the religion. For example, the declaration expressly forbids the State to coerce a citizen into the confession of a particular creed. At the same time it upholds the noble teaching that only the free conscience can make a true profession of faith.[34] Citizens may not be compelled to adopt the faith under any circumstances. At a glance, this appears to be a change in attitude from the position previously held by the Church, which had always insisted on the public profession of Christ's social kingship—particularly through the voice of Leo XIII.

We will return to the issue of Church and State at the appropriate point in our study,[35] but for now it suffices to quote a section from *Dignitatis Humanae* which is all too often disregarded, but which points us in the direction of clarity as to the Council's intent:

> "Religious freedom...has to do with immunity from coercion in civil society. Therefore it leaves untouched traditional Catholic doctrine on the moral duty of men and societies toward the true religion and toward the one Church of Christ."[36]

Now, taking what we already said above regarding the relationship between Church and State,[37] and if we also admit that *Dignitatis Humanae* does contain statements which would seem to contradict "traditional Catholic doctrine," we must choose between three possible ways of handling the situation:

1. We can ignore the quote above, take the *apparent departure* from tradition as a *real departure* from tradition, side with tradition, reject the document, the council, and all post-conciliar popes, and thereby

---

[34] *DH*, 2.

[35] Link to the part.

[36] *DH*, 1.

[37] Section I, 1b.

separate ourselves from the Church as it exists today. This option corresponds with the so called "sedevacantists."

2. We can ignore the quote above, take the *apparent departure* from tradition as *real departure* from tradition, side *against* tradition, thereby separating ourselves from two-thousand years of Church teachings. This is the position of the liberal or "modernist" elements of the Church.

3. We can take the quote above into full account, giving the Magisterium the benefit of the doubt which it deserves, assuming that it would not so blatantly contradict itself. We can then set ourselves to the task of reconciling the *apparent* contradiction between *Dignitatis Humanae* and the traditional understanding on religious liberty, such as the one taught by Leo XIII in *Immortale Dei* and *Libertas*. (Both of Leo XIII's encyclicals, we might add, are cited in *Dignitatis Humanae*.) For example, we can assume that a State may be forbidden to coerce belief while at one and the same time being obligated to acknowledge Christ as King.

We will adopt the third approach throughout this study. Any other way of going about things would make this project, and any other of its kind, a waste of effort. How exactly this reconciliation of an apparent contradiction must be handled will become clear in what follows, particularly in Section VI, part 4.

6. Catholic Social Teaching, systems, and ideology

Because of the constant need to re-interpret and re-apply the principles of its social doctrine, *which are themselves unchanging*, it should be obvious that the Church will never present a specific economic "system" or political "program" of any kind.[38] Technical applications are not, and cannot be, its domain, since they must be built and modified according to the unique circumstances of each historical, geographical, and cultural situation. Technical solutions that prove fruitful for one social

---

[38] *CV*, 10.

group or geographical zone may prove inappropriate for another, and so it would be futile for the Church to try and produce a "one-size-fits-all" solution and demand that its solution be blindly applied to all peoples at all times. Such is the danger of ideological thinking, which the Church avoids at all times. However, it should also be said that precisely due to the fact that the Church stands beyond ideology and specific systems, she retains the ability to judge the appropriateness of these systems, as to whether or not they meet the requirements of her principles. This means that when the Church denounces capitalism and socialism, it remains within its rights; and it can denounce these illegitimate systems without having to offer an alternative "system" to be erected in their place. Discernment and principles are her domain. What she claims to offer is "an indispensable and ideal orientation,"[39] which she calls upon the laity to put into practice, each in his own sphere of competence according to his vocation.

7. Authority of the Doctrine

It is also good to mention that, when it comes to works such as the one you have before you, as well as when considering official documents such as the *Compendium* and the *Catechism*, the citations used will differ in rank with respect to authority. There are papal addresses, encyclicals and council documents, as well as the occasional work produced by conferences of bishops such as the *USCCB*. Even within council documents there are varying degrees of authority between constitutions, declarations, and decrees.[40]

While it would be possible to elaborate on the binding force of each type of document, detailing the degree of assent demanded from the believer who wishes to remain in good standing, we choose not to enter into that subject here. The reason for this approach can be found in the social conditions prevalent in our era. We have already hinted above at these conditions. Within modern liberal-democratic regimes such as the United States, the social mind tends to be preoccupied with *freedom*

---

[39] *CA*, 43.
[40] *CSDC*, 8.

from religious authority, rather than with *duty toward* it. The result is that appeals to authority, whether legitimate or not, fail to exert any force whatsoever on contemporary audiences. Listeners instinctively turn against any claims on their conscience which are not chosen solely by themselves. The principle of *docility,* or the suggestions that a person can adopt a posture of submission while retaining his dignity, simply does not compute in cultures where each person is assured, from the cradle to the grave, that there is no higher authority than his own reason or preference, and that he owes obedience to no one. Thus, we have judged it prudent in this work to pass over an examination of the binding nature of certain documents, proceeding on to the teachings themselves in hopes that, although we will make no attempt to prove their varying degrees of authority, the reader will be sufficiently interested in the doctrines that he will explore the matter himself.

Moreover, by openly avoiding the legalistic paradigm of what one must and must not believe, we are able to outline the body of social teachings more comprehensively, because much of it consists, not in laying out what the church demands, but, as we said above, in indicating the lofty ideal *for which it hopes,* and after which we are obliged, as lovers of Christ, to strive.

Section II. The Truth About Man

1. His social nature

We have already said that man is neither body nor soul, but is at the same time *body-and-soul*. We must now add to this another truth. While the first went against the grain of contemporary materialism, this second truth flies in the face of our pervasive individualism: "God did not create man as a 'solitary being' but wished him to be a 'social being'. Social life therefore is not exterior to man: he can only grow and realize his vocation in relation with others."[41] The human person is called from the very beginning to lead a social life: "It is not good for man to be alone."[42]

Being made in the image and likeness of the triune God, the human person is naturally communal and distinguished from other creatures in this respect. The Church proclaims this truth about man constantly, and all of CST presupposes it.[43] Even in addressing issues of a purely economic concern, the need for communion is kept central. As Benedict XVI stated:

> "One of the deepest forms of poverty a person can experience is isolation. If we look closely at other kinds of poverty, including material forms, we see that they are born from isolation, from not being loved or from difficulties in being able to love."[44]

a. Aquinas on the social nature of man

In his epistle, *De Regno*, St. Thomas provides various arguments for this position which are worth listing here due to their simplicity and coherence.

---

[41] *LC*, 32.

[42] *Gen* 2:18.

[43] See also: *GS*, 12; *CCC*, 1879; *PT*, 23; *LP*, 10.

[44] *CV*, 53.

i. Man is physically unsuited for survival in isolation. "For all other animals, nature has prepared food, hair as a covering, teeth, horns, claws as means of defence or at least speed in flight, while man alone was made without any natural provisions for these things. Instead of all these, man was endowed with reason, by the use of which he could procure all these things for himself by the work of his hands. Now, one man alone is not able to procure them all for himself, for one man could not sufficiently provide for life, unassisted. It is therefore natural that man should live in the society of many."[45]

ii. Man lacks the sufficiency of instinct found in other creatures. "All other animals are able to, discern, by inborn skill, what is useful and what is injurious, even as the sheep naturally regards the wolf as his enemy. Some animals also recognize by natural skill certain medicinal herbs and other things necessary for their life. Man, on the contrary, has a natural knowledge of the things which are essential for his life only in a general fashion, inasmuch as he is able to attain knowledge of the particular things necessary for human life by reasoning from natural principles. But it is not possible for one man to arrive at a knowledge of all these things by his own individual reason. It is therefore necessary for man to live in a multitude so that each one may assist his fellows, and different men may be occupied in seeking, by their reason, to make different discoveries—one, for example, in medicine, one in this and another in that."[46]

iii. Through the gift of speech man is made for communication. "...the use of speech is a prerogative proper to man. By this means, one man is able fully to express his conceptions to others. Other animals, it is true, express their feelings to one another in a general way, as a dog may express anger by barking and other animals give vent to other feelings in various fashions. But man communicates

---

[45] *DR*, 5.
[46] *DR*, 6.

with his kind more completely than any other animal known to be gregarious, such as the crane, the ant or the bee. With this in mind, Solomon says: 'It is better that there be two than one; for they have the advantage of their company.' "[47]

b. The consensus of the pagans

This truth about man was acknowledged in the pagan world as well. Aristotle had proclaimed that "man is by nature a political animal," which he follows by quoting Homer, who said that any man who lives outside of the community of other persons does so, not because he is acting according to human nature, but because he is either below or above humanity. He is either an ascetic or a villain—and both of these are, of course, exceptions which serve to prove the rule.[48]

c. The Enlightenment and the "social contract"

What has been said so far leaves little room for the so-called "libertarian" mentality, which would conceive of man as a "noble savage" who enters into society only as a necessary evil rather than as a natural good. Such a view, although it seems quite normal today, is quite modern and is in fact a product of Enlightenment humanism. Only during that period did it become a core doctrine, eventually evolving into the school of thought known as Liberalism. If, taking a wider view, we survey human history in general, we find that this anti-social point of view is quite in the minority. If we survey Christian history specifically, we find that it is non-existent.

d. Personal development

We are warned never to lose sight of the interdependence of man and his fellows. "The human person may never be thought of only as an absolute individual being, built up by himself and on himself."[49] If we are to consider personal growth and realization in its fullness, we must be able to acknowledge the role of personal responsibility in the

---

[47] DR, 7.
[48] Aristotle, *Politics*, Book I, part 2.
[49] CSDC, 125.

development of the individual, while at the same time taking into account our profound need for community. Pope Benedict XVI elaborated on the paradox:

> "The human person by nature is actively involved in his own development…since as everybody knows, we are all capable of making free and responsible choices. Nor is it merely at the mercy of our caprice, since we all know that we are a gift, not something self-generated. Our freedom is profoundly shaped by our being, and by its limits. No one shapes his own conscience arbitrarily, but we all build our own 'I' on the basis of a 'self' which is given to us. Not only are other persons outside our control, but each one of us is outside his or her own control. A person's development is compromised, if he claims to be solely responsible for producing what he becomes."[50]

e. Social sin

Although CST does not spend a great deal of time developing the theological understanding of sin, it necessarily takes it into account as it pertains to the subject. What this means is that CST acknowledges not only the personal aspect of sin, but also its social aspect. It teaches that "every sin is social insofar as and because it also has social consequences."[51] While sin is a result of the personal actions of an individual's free will, yet by virtue of human solidarity every sin of the individual directly impacts his neighbor. This is not by any means an attempt to cancel the responsibility of the individual sinner, but is rather, as was suggested above, an examination of sinfulness from its interpersonal aspect, which complements its individual aspect.

f. The law of descent—the law of ascent

To express the same thing in terms used by St. John Paul II, we can say that as a consequence of the social aspect of sin it is appropriate to speak of a "law of descent" which is a kind of "communion of sin" by which

---

[50] *CV,* 68.
[51] *CSDC,* 117.

each sinful soul drags down the whole Church along with it. On the bright side, this also implies a corresponding "law of ascent" which operates by virtue of the "communion of saints," and so it is said that "every soul that rises above itself, raises up the world."[52]

The body of Christ is a unity that hangs together, for better or worse, in solidarity unto the end. It is precisely this social reality which informs the Catholic principle of solidarity which we will discuss below. For if our lives are intertwined, and if it is easier to live virtuously when material conditions are at an optimum level, then we ought to do our utmost to lift our neighbors from want, and we ought to see clearly that our own prosperity is not enough.

2. Rights and Duties

We proceed next to the notion of "right," and this for two reasons. First, because it is a word that is on the tip of every tongue these days and so it seems reasonable to address the most familiar and pressing issues first. This will allow us to iron out any misconceptions that may exist, and clear the way for other issues that may have been obscured by the confusion. Second, we address the issue of right because it is directly linked to man's social nature, which is to say: *rights are social.*

Specific applications will be avoided at this point in favor of a few general observations about the nature of the right. For example, we will forgo the discussion of individual rights (such as those pertaining to life, speech, worship, etc.) until they present themselves naturally in the course of our study.

a. Rights imply relation

St. Thomas Aquinas said that "right is the object of justice."[53] It is here that we can see the social or *relational* aspect of the right, since justice implies two parties. Insofar as a man is bound by justice, he is bound in a relationship, even if we reduce this relationship to its most primordial

---

[52] *RP*, 16.
[53] *ST* II-II, q. 57, a. 1.

level, such as the original relation between creature and Creator. What follows from this observation is that there is really no such thing as a purely "individual" right which one claims for oneself against the claims of others and which is owed to him absolutely without distinction and unconditionally. Just as there are two parties in the relationship, there are two aspects of justice, and the right is only one of them—the other aspect being *duty*. If duty is neglected, the concept of right is undermined from the start. Nicholas Gomez-Davila struck at the heart of this confusion when he lamented: "It has become customary to proclaim rights in order to be able to violate duties."[54] To violate one's own duty is automatically to violate the rights of another.

b. Rights presuppose duties

The Catholic Church always addresses the notion of right and duty at the same time. The former cannot be separated from the latter without undermining both. Following the reasoning of St. John XXIII, we can say that rights "are inextricably bound up with as many duties, all applying to one and the same person. These rights and duties derive their origin, their sustenance, and their indestructibility from the natural law, which in conferring the one imposes the other."[55] To use but one example, we can say that the right to life carries with it the duty to preserve one's life. The two components are two sides of the same coin: "to claim one's rights and ignore one's duties, or only half fulfill them, is like building a house with one hand and tearing it down with the other."[56] This is why the Church, sensing an unfortunate "gap" between the *letter* and the *spirit* of rights,[57] calls for the constant fostering of a social sense that remains aware of the needs of the common good.[58]

---

[54] *Scholia to an Implicit Text*, 2587.

[55] *PT*, 28.

[56] *PT*, 30.

[57] *RH*, 17.

[58] *OA*, 23.

c. Rights are not absolute

From this we can surmise that rights are not to be considered absolute. The Church calls them "inalienable," which is to say, they are derived from human nature, but their *exercise* must always be circumscribed within limits. They are "contingent." To take but one common example, the Church has consistently proclaimed the right to private property, and yet the *Compendium* says plainly that "*Christian tradition has never recognized the right to private property as absolute and untouchable.*"[59] It will be appropriate to elaborate further on this particular point when we arrive at our discussion of private property below. For now, we need only illustrate that the notion of "right" is a balance, and is just as much directed outward, toward neighbor, as it is inward, toward the self. Rights must never become captive to a self-centered, egoistic paradigm if they are to remain healthy and functional.

3. Family Life

Having begun by acknowledging the social nature of man, we may proceed naturally to the most primordial of societies, which is the family. The family is the center of CST, but in order to grasp its importance we must first understand its parts. This leads inevitably to a discussion of man and wife, which confronts us with the reality of gender—of man as "man and woman."

a. Male and female "from the beginning"

"Haven't you read that in the beginning the Creator made them male and female?"[60] From Christ's words to the Pharisees, St. John Paul II infers in his *Theology of the Body* that we have little reason to consider man simply *as man*, but that we should instead always consider man as "male and female."[61] Here he is drawing a distinction between historical man and man in the state of innocence, which, for St. John Paul II, was a primordial and therefore pre-historical state.

---

[59] *CSDC*, 177.

[60] *Mt* 19:4.

[61] *Man and Woman He Created Them: A Theology of the Body* (Boston, 2006), pp. 132-133.

The saint observes that the first chapter of Genesis is *objective*, while the second is *subjective*. In the objective account (Genesis 1) the scriptures, taking the perspective of God, do not speak of "man" as anything other than "male and female." Thus, from God's point of view, neither of the sexes precedes or follows the other, but both are created together "from the beginning."[62]

The second account, on the other hand (Genesis 2), is *subjective*, which is to say, it is the story of creation *from man's point of view*. It dwells on what St. John Paul II termed the "original experiences" of man which go to constitute and explain the human condition. Genesis 2 conveys these primordial happenings in a way that is comprehensible to us. This is why the second account has the character of myth and is essentially supra-historical (although not necessarily non-historical).[63]

Fallen man is "historical man." His experience of life is valid only as far back as historical man has existed—but this does not and cannot reach into the pre-historical period of innocence. Such is the justification for and the purpose of the creation myth, with the result that, although it relates its details through a chronological scheme in which the male precedes the female, it must be interpreted first and foremost as conveying an ontological ordering of creation rather than an actual ordering of events in time.

The conclusion of all this is that we are not equipped to speak either *historically* or *experientially* of man without taking into account his relation to woman. This fundamental bifurcation is indispensable and unavoidable: there is no such thing as a genderless "person." We must always follow Christ and speak of man as male and female "from the beginning." Female-ness (and male-ness, for that matter) was not an afterthought based on God's failed attempt to create a single, happy, gender-neutral human being.

---

[62] Ibid., pp. 134-136.
[63] Ibid., pp. 137-141.

In fact, the proper interpretation of Genesis is born out linguistically in the account itself. When the narrative speaks of the "original experiences"—such as the "original loneliness"—of Adam before the creation of woman, it employs a word which means mankind in general, without reference to gender. Thus, everything that is said of Adam before the creation of Eve must, to a certain extent, describe the experiences of mankind as a whole—including those of women. That is to say, women also have an experiential connection with the "original loneliness" felt by Adam ("mankind in general") before the creation of Eve.

Thus, if we are not justified in considering mankind as one gender or the other, or as some abstract, genderless "person," but instead must always consider mankind as the ambiguously complementary gendered dualism, and if we acknowledge that this dualism inevitably produces a third being from within itself (the child), then we come immediately to the family as a fundamental human reality, which is a single unit in love—an earthly reflection of the Triune God.

b. The cell of society—the cradle of life

Just as God is a Trinity, and cannot be considered as three separate Gods each going separate ways, so the fundamental social unit is the family, and not the individual as father, mother or child.[64] The family is the basic unit of political and economic organization in the Catholic tradition. As an association, it is prior to every other. "It is in this cradle of life and love that people are born and grow."[65] Here the person takes his first steps into his personhood, learns responsibility, and develops his manifold potentialities. The family is the "fundamental structure for human ecology."[66]

---

[64] *LS*, 157.
[65] *CSDC*, 212.
[66] *CA*, 39.

Because man is fundamentally a social being, it can be said that "only insofar as he understands himself in reference to a 'thou' can he say 'I'." It is in the family that he "comes out of himself, from the self-centred preservation of his own life, to enter into a relationship of dialogue and communion with others."[67] This is why no law can threaten this institution—the State exists for the family and not the family for the State.

> "No human law can abolish the natural and original right of marriage, nor in any way limit the chief and original purpose of marriage, ordained by God's authority from the beginning. Increase and multiply. Hence we have the Family; the 'society' of a man's house—a society limited indeed in numbers, but no less a true society, anterior to every kind of State or Nation, invested with rights and duties of its own, totally independent of the civil community...Inasmuch as the domestic household is antecedent, as well in idea as in fact, to the gathering of men into a community, the Family must necessarily have rights and duties which are prior to those of the community, and founded more immediately in nature...The contention then, that the civil government should at its option intrude into and exercise intimate control over the Family and the household, is a great and pernicious error."[68]

Pius XI affirmed this teaching in *Casti Connubii*, referring to marriage as "the principle and foundation of domestic society, and therefore of all human intercourse."[69]

c. The domestic Church

St. John Paul II, in his Apostolic Exhortation, *Familiaris Consortio*, goes further and establishes that the Family is in fact an active unit in the mission of the Church. He calls it an *Ecclesia domestica* or "Church in miniature" which is "in its own way...a living image and historical

---

[67] *CSDC*, 130; See also: *LS*, 213.
[68] *RN*, 12-14.
[69] *CC*, 1.

representation of the mystery of the Church."[70] The Family is thus a "little Church,"[71] a "domestic Church,"[72] the "Church of the home,"[73] which is "grafted" into the mystery of the Church proper and is therefore a sharer in its mission; and so, while it is true that the family has been present always and everywhere, through Christ it has been baptized and made *transcendent.*

The family constitutes a "specific revelation" of the mind and purpose of God. In it and through it the highest forms of human communion are realized and presented to the world as a prophetic "sign of unity"—as such, the family is truly a "school of deeper humanity"[74] because in it are practiced all the acts of daily kindness: care for young and old alike, forbearance, forgiveness, and self-giving. Every part of the person is called into play and perfected.

d. Two-fold purpose of the family

After establishing the primacy of the family in Catholic tradition, we can emphasize that the importance of the family rests on its dual purpose: 1) It exists to fulfill the divine command to continue the race—"Be fruitful and multiply." 2) It meets the basic human need of a close community in which love is paramount.

It must be remembered, however, that while both functions are essential, they must be kept in the order just given. Slight deviations in first principles are responsible for grave deviations in their applications. The propagation of children is the *first purpose* of marriage; conjugal and parental love is the *second.* This is but a consistent application of the principle set forth at the beginning of this study, that *grace presupposes nature*, and that the higher things in life require at least a bare minimum of the lower. Regardless of how noble the emotionally

---

[70] *FC,* 49.

[71] *FC,* 86.

[72] *FC,* 21.

[73] *FC,* 38.

[74] *FC,* 21.

and personally edifying aspects of the marriage relationship might be, its natural basis is prior and is the foundation which cannot be removed without undermining the whole thing.

Moreover, we should note that the family is a biological necessity for mankind even more so than animals, whose offspring often need little to no support before reaching developmental independence. Man's higher vocation implies a greater natural dependence in order for that vocation to develop, and this development occurs within the family.

This specific call to domestic life, as opposed to the simple act of reproduction, is a peculiar need for mankind. St. Thomas declares that: "The human male and female are united, not only for generation, as with other animals, but also for the purpose of domestic life, in which each has his or her particular duty."[75] And he tenderly amplifies the same point elsewhere: "Before it has the use of its free-will, [the child] is enfolded in the care of its parents, which is like a spiritual womb."[76]

If the importance of the family has not been made undeniably clear from what has already been said, then we need only meditate on the fact that Christ Himself remained concealed within this spiritual womb until the age of thirty, and it was only then that he began his public ministry. If it was deemed proper that the Savior should make full and good use of this institution, then we should probably not underestimate its formative power.

e. The needs of the family are central to CST

Here we must refer once more to the indispensable principle that *grace presupposes nature*, ensuring that we apply it comprehensively. Indeed it is impossible to over-stress this particular truth, and it is precisely the neglect of this truth which has led to numerous perversions of the social order. With regard to CST, the application of this principle means that the lofty and diverse duties of the family cannot be carried out in an

---

[75] *ST* I, q. 92, a. 2.
[76] *ST* II-II, q. 10, a. 12.

economic vacuum. The family requires for its normal and healthy functioning a certain sufficiency of material goods. If we desire stable families, we require a stable economic substrate within which they can grow and thrive. It is ridiculous to complain, as some have made a habit of doing, that the family is decaying in its moral aspects, while at the same time refusing to make any provisions for its material aspects. Such an attitude turns its own complaint into a self-fulfilling prophecy. Divorce, absentee fathers, and abortion undoubtedly undermine virtue and human flourishing, and are rightfully condemned; but it is undeniable that poverty and insecurity are primary causes of such moral failures. It is short-sightedness pure and simple to condemn the deterioration of virtue while ignoring the economic structures that jeopardize the economic stability of the family, which acts as the training ground of virtue.

Section III. Permanent Principles

Having allowed the Church, as an "expert in humanity,"[77] to inform our view of the family as the basis of human society, we can now turn to those "universal principles" which it was claimed earlier that only the Church is competent to provide. On these principles, which are universal guides rather than specific cultural and political applications, we must build the remainder of our study.

1. Common Good

Having acknowledged that man is social by nature, we can reasonably conclude that all aspects of social life must be related to the *common good*.[78] The whole is indeed greater than the part.[79] This is not to be construed as a disavowal of the individual in favor of the collective, but is rather a concern for the community, as a *perfect society*, that it may serve the needs of each individual, providing the conditions he requires for the full realization of his potential. The individual is not less than the community, but because he requires the community for his development, he depends upon it, and because he depends upon it he has a duty to seek its preservation. Each man is obligated to show concern for the common good, and to contribute to it as he is able. It would be flatly contradictory to operate on the premise that, although his proper fulfillment is found in society, he ought to consider his actions only in their individual aspect. There is no room in CST for the individualist mentality.[80]

It must also be mentioned that the obligation to care for the common good extends not only through space but also through time. There must be justice between generations. The Jeffersonian motto that "the land belongs only to the living" finds no echo in the Church, which demands that our immediate concerns "cannot exclude those who come after us."[81]

---

[77] *PP*, 13.
[78] *CSDC*, 164.
[79] *LS*, 141; *EG*, 247.
[80] *EG*, 67, 78, 89, 99; *OA*, 23.

The earth "is on loan to each generation, which must then hand it on to the next."[82] Through this principle we are called to practice "intergenerational solidarity."[83]

2. Universal Destination of Goods

As a direct consequence of the principle of the common good, we arrive at the universal destination of goods. In the words of the Second Vatican Council: "God destined the earth and all it contains for all men and all peoples so that all created things would be shared fairly by all mankind under the guidance of justice tempered by charity."[84] The earth—that first and greatest gift of nature from God to man—is the perennial source of sustenance to the human race, and because no man can do without the material goods that fulfill his basic needs (food and shelter), there exists a primordial right to use of its resources.[85]

3. Private Property

Continuing in our logical progression, we come to private property, of which the first thing to be said is that it is a *consequence* of the universal destination of goods. As such it should never be imagined as something antagonistic to it or separate from it, as if the two principles operated in opposition to one another. They are mutually complementary and supportive. According to Aquinas:

"Community of goods is ascribed to the natural law, not that the natural law dictates that all things should be possessed in common and that nothing should be possessed as one's own: but because the division of possessions is not according to the natural law, but rather arose from human agreement which belongs to positive

---

[81] *LS*, 158.

[82] Portuguese Bishops' Conference, *Responsabilidade Solidária pelo Bem Comum* (15 September 2003), 20.

[83] *LS*, 159.

[84] *GS*, 69.

[85] *CCC*, 2402, 2452; *CSDC*, 176-181; *CA*, 6; *RN*, 22.

law...Hence the ownership of possessions is not contrary to the natural law, but an addition thereto devised by human reason."[86]

What Aquinas illustrates here is the Church's notion of a "hierarchy of goods." That everyone ought to have the opportunity to share in the goods of the earth is a dictate of natural law, but since the best way of achieving the widespread and responsible use of goods does not lie in communal ownership, we choose instead to implement the institution of private property. Private property is a good which is "superimposed" on top of the universal destination of goods in order to best serve it. Thus, private property must be conceived *as a means* of achieving an end:

> "The fact that God has given the earth for the use and enjoyment of the whole human race can in no way be a bar to the owning of private property. For God has granted the earth to mankind in general, not in the sense that all without distinction can deal with it as they like, but rather that no part of it was assigned to any one in particular, and that the limits of private possession have been left to be fixed by man's own industry, and by the laws of individual races. Moreover, the earth, even though apportioned among private owners, ceases not thereby to minister to the needs of all, inasmuch as there is not one who does not sustain life from what the land produces."[87]

a. Justifications for private property according to Aquinas

Aquinas provides three concise reasons for the above, with which we would be wise to arm ourselves. First, every man is more careful to procure what is for himself alone than that which is common to many or to all. Second, human affairs are conducted more orderly if each man is charged with taking care of some particular thing himself. Third, we know that a more peaceful state is ensured to man if each one is contented with his own.[88]

---

[86] *ST* II-II, q. 66, a. 2, ad. 1.
[87] *RN*, 8.

b. The right of private property is to support the family

Because the family, rather than the individual, is the basic unit of society, then it must be acknowledged that the institution of private property is valid if and only if it benefits the family first and foremost, ensuring its stability and contributing to its development.

> "It is a most sacred law of nature that a father should provide food and all necessaries for those whom he has begotten; and, similarly, it is natural that he should wish that his children, who carry on, so to speak, and continue his personality, should be by him provided with all that is needful to enable them to keep themselves decently from want and misery amid the uncertainties of this mortal life. Now, in no other way can a father effect this except by the ownership of productive property, which he can transmit to his children by inheritance."[89]

If conditions arise such that private property is somehow appropriated by individuals while families are left either without property or dependent on a few rich individuals for their survival, then it would become clear that private property was no longer serving its end, and it would open itself to just criticism.

c. The right of private property is not absolute

St. John Paul II said that "there is always a social mortgage on all private property, in order that goods may serve the general purpose that God gave them."[90]

Obviously this means that the right of private property is not absolute.[91] Indeed, Pope Francis has said that "God rejects every claim to absolute ownership."[92] The universal destination of goods is always God's point

---

[88] *ST* II-II, q. 66, a. 2.

[89] *RN*, 13.

[90] *Address to Indigenous and Rural People*, Cuilapán, Mexico (29 January 1979), 6.

[91] *LS*, 93; CSDC, 177.

of departure.[93] Whenever circumstances arise in which private property comes into conflict with this principle, for example, if those who have an abundance of goods are unwilling to assist those in need, then it is quite legitimate for the State to intervene. In fact, because it is the role of the State to see to the just establishment and distribution of social goods, it would be irresponsible for it to remain silent. Far from being an offense against private property, such actions may become necessary in order to maintain the institution by protecting it from abuse. Aquinas himself went even further, saying: "All things are common property in a case of extreme necessity. Hence one who is in such dire straits may take another's goods in order to succour himself, if he can find no one who is willing to give him something."[94] Although such a position sounds extreme, the *Catechism* is in agreement.[95]

4. The preferential option for the poor

Pope Leo XIII instructed the State to show preference to social groups depending on the amount of political and economic power they were capable of wielding on their own behalf. That is to say, the State owes special attention to the weakest elements of society:

> "The richer class have many ways of shielding themselves, and stand less in need of help from the State; whereas the mass of the poor have no resources of their own to fall back upon, and must chiefly depend upon the assistance of the State."[96]

Particularly when speaking of the market, this means that it will sometimes be necessary to place stronger restraints on the actions of those with greater resources in order to ensure that the so-called "free market" remains free:

---

[92] *LS*, 67.
[93] *LE*, 14.
[94] *ST* II-II, q. 32, a. 7.
[95] *CCC*, 2408.
[96] *RN*, 37.

"To ensure economic freedom from which all can effectively benefit, restraints occasionally have to be imposed on those possessing greater resources and financial power. To claim economic freedom while real conditions bar many people from actual access to it, and while possibilities for employment continue to shrink, is to practise a doublespeak which brings politics into disrepute."[97]

Because this responsibility is explicitly assigned to the State, we will develop this notion further when we arrive at our discussion of political society.[98]

5. Solidarity and Subsidiarity

Solidarity and subsidiarity go to form a pair of principles which, much like right and duty, should not be considered as separate or opposed, but rather as two sides of a coin which go to create a complementary harmony. Because of their correspondence, we have grouped them under the same heading. In fact, just as right destroys itself if divorced from the concept of duty, so subsidiarity and solidarity are guaranteed to destroy themselves if taken in isolation. That is why, as a general rule of thumb, we ought to be wary of any politician or reformer who claims to be a firm believer in one of these principles if he seems to neglect the other. He who does not grasp the interdependence of the pair will inevitably upset the balance of justice:

> "*The principle of subsidiarity must remain closely linked to the principle of solidarity and vice versa*, since the former without the latter gives way to social privatism, while the latter without the former gives way to paternalist social assistance that is demeaning to those in need."[99]

Having stressed their relation, we can proceed to discuss the unique truth represented by each.

---

[97] *LS*, 129.
[98] See Section VI below.
[99] *CV*, 58.

a. Solidarity—working for the common good

St. Paul says in the Scriptures that we are one body, and that "if one member suffer anything, all the members suffer with it; or if one member glory, all the members rejoice with it."[100] The principle of solidarity is nothing more than the acknowledgement of this truth. It is not shallow sentimentalism; it is the acknowledgment of a responsibility: "[Solidarity] is not a feeling of vague compassion or shallow distress at the misfortunes of so many people, both near and far. On the contrary, it is a firm and persevering determination to commit oneself to the common good; that is to say, to the good of all and of each individual, because we are all really responsible for all."[101] "It is precisely in this sense that Cain's answer to the Lord's question: 'Where is Abel your brother?' can be interpreted: 'I do not know; am I my brother's keeper?' (Gen 4:9). Yes, every man is his 'brother's keeper', because God entrusts us to one another."[102] However, even though there is an undeniable aspect of obligation in the principle of solidarity, at its core it is an expression of love, because to love another is to desire their good and to be willing to act in order to secure it.[103]

b. Subsidiarity—enabling responsibility

Described by the popes as an effort to achieve a "graduated order"[104] and to encourage the "stratified"[105] organization of social institutions, subsidiarity promotes the teaching that man has a role to play in both private and public life, and ought to be allowed to play it insofar as he is capable of doing so.

> i. **Subsidiarity as a response to doctrinaire individualism.** We must be wary of subsidiarity as abused by the libertarian ideology. It is not, as has been frequently construed, meant to be an affirmation of

---

[100] Cf. *1 Cor* 12:12-26.

[101] *SRS*, 38.

[102] *EV*, 19.

[103] *CV*, 7.

[104] *QA*, 80.

[105] *CV*, 57.

individualism. In fact, if we trace the development of subsidiarity in CST, we find that it was originally formulated as a response to the evils that *pervasive individualism*[106] had brought about:

> "When we speak of the reform of institutions, the State comes chiefly to mind, not as if universal well-being were to be expected from its activity, but because things have come to such a pass through the evil of what we have termed 'individualism' that, following upon the overthrow and near extinction of that rich social life which was once highly developed through associations of various kinds, there remain virtually only individuals and the State. This is to the great harm of the State itself; for, with a structure of social governance lost, and with the taking over of all the burdens which the wrecked associations once bore, the State has been overwhelmed and crushed by almost infinite tasks and duties."[107]

This passage illustrates the point that even sound principles, if pushed to an extreme limit, will sooner or later turn into their opposite. This has certainly proven true in the case of individualism, which, as we have just seen, is actually the *cause of* rather than the *answer to* the growth of the paternal State.

ii. Subsidiarity defined. Thus, subsidiarity represents an answer to the dual problem of individualism and collectivism, meant to act as a harmonizing principle between autonomy and unity:

> "Just as it is gravely wrong to take from individuals what they can accomplish by their own initiative and industry and give it to the community, so also it is an injustice and at the same time a grave evil and disturbance of right order to assign to a greater and higher association what lesser and subordinate organizations can do. For every social activity ought of its very

---

[106] See also: *LS*, 119, 162, 208, 210.
[107] *QA*, 78.

nature to furnish help to the members of the body social, and never destroy and absorb them."[108]

iii. Subsidiarity enables the State to act in its proper sphere. Only if the principle of subsidiarity is acted upon will States themselves be able to focus on those areas in which they are most competent:

> "The supreme authority of the State ought, therefore, to let subordinate groups handle matters and concerns of lesser importance, which would otherwise dissipate its efforts greatly. Thereby the State will more freely, powerfully, and effectively do all those things that belong to it alone because it alone can do them: directing, watching, urging, restraining, as occasion requires and necessity demands."[109]

iii. Geared toward the family and intermediate associations. It is worth noting once more that CST rarely addresses men as individuals. Even when protecting his autonomy, the Church speaks in such a way that his social nature is affirmed rather than denied. Thus, the principle of subsidiarity itself is geared, not toward individuals, but toward associations, so that these small communities—the first and foremost being the family—can act responsibly without being "subsumed" by larger bodies.[110] The overarching idea is not that man ought to be more atomized, which is the tendency of individualism, but that he ought to be free to associate effectively and in a personal, responsible fashion with his peers:

> "Subsidiarity is first and foremost a form of assistance to the human person via the autonomy of intermediate bodies. Such assistance is offered when individuals or groups are unable to accomplish something on their own, and it is always designed to

---

[108] *QA*, 79.
[109] *QA*, 80.
[110] *RN*, 35.

achieve their emancipation, because it fosters freedom and participation through assumption of responsibility. Subsidiarity respects personal dignity by recognizing in the person a subject who is always capable of giving something to others. By considering reciprocity as the heart of what it is to be a human being, subsidiarity is the most effective antidote against any form of all-encompassing welfare state."[111]

6. Freedom

Arriving now at the subject of freedom and its role in the social teachings of the Church, we can begin by repeating a saying of St. John Paul II: "Freedom consists not in doing what we like, but in having the right to do what we ought."[112] Within this simple motto is a treasure-trove of meaning.

---

[111] *CV,* 57.

[112] St. John Paul II's words are worth citing in greater depth, as he is speaking in America and to Americans: "One hundred thirty years ago, President Abraham Lincoln asked whether a nation 'conceived in liberty and dedicated to the proposition that all men are created equal' could 'long endure'. President Lincoln's question is no less a question for the present generation of Americans. Democracy cannot be sustained without a shared commitment to certain moral truths about the human person and human community. The basic question before a democratic society is: 'how ought we to live together?' In seeking an answer to this question, can society exclude moral truth and moral reasoning? Can the Biblical wisdom which played such a formative part in the very founding of your country be excluded from that debate? Would not doing so mean that America's founding documents no longer have any defining content, but are only the formal dressing of changing opinion? Would not doing so mean that tens of millions of Americans could no longer offer the contribution of their deepest convictions to the formation of public policy? Surely it is important for America that the moral truths which make freedom possible should be passed on to each new generation. Every generation of Americans needs to know that freedom consists not in doing what we like, but in having the right to do what we ought." *Homily given at Oriole Park at Camden Yards,* Baltimore on October 8, 1995, 7.

First, that freedom should not be understood merely as the arbitrary exercise of the individual's will, but that it consists in the ability to direct one's will toward a certain end—the good. This means that freedom is *purposive*, which is to say *teleological*. But even if we acknowledge the nature of freedom as having a specific direction, we immediately run up against another question: how is one to know which direction is right? We then come to understand how knowledge is a necessary prerequisite to the healthy exercise of freedom. We finally realize why man is the only "free" creature—because freedom requires intelligence and the choice to act in accordance with the truth gained thereby. Here lies the essence of human responsibility. Man can be free because he can seek truth, adhere to it, and act upon it.

a. Purposive freedom

Freedom is neither an end nor an absolute. Its legitimacy is contingent on its vector—on how it is directed—and any formulation that divorces it from its directional aspect also destroys its validity. The Second Vatican Council put it thus:

> "God willed to leave man in the power of his own counsel, so that he would seek his Creator of his own accord and would freely arrive at full and blessed perfection by cleaving to God."[113]

In saying this we acknowledge not only that freedom has a direction, but we acknowledge also its proper goal, which is communion with God.[114] These characteristics temper the mentality, all too prevalent today, that in order to consider ourselves free we must also consider ourselves *separate* from the influence of our fellows. On the contrary, authentic freedom "is acquired in *love,* that is, in the *gift of self.*"[115] Likewise it balances a second tendency of the same mentality, which would prefer a freedom almost without limits and which is also contrary to the Catholic understanding of the matter:

---

[113] *GS,* 17.
[114] *VS,* 86.
[115] *VS,* 87.

"That freedom is real but limited: its absolute and unconditional origin is not in itself, but in the life within which it is situated and which represents for it, at one and the same time, both a limitation and a possibility. Human freedom belongs to us as creatures; it is a freedom which is given as a gift, one to be received like a seed and to be cultivated responsibly."[116]

b. Freedom of the will depends on intelligence

As we have already suggested, human liberty presupposes intelligence. "Liberty...belongs only to those who have the gift of reason or intelligence. Considered as to its nature, it is the faculty of choosing means fitted for the end proposed, for he is master of his actions who can choose one thing out of many."[117] And so there can be no freedom—of will or anything else—without the human power to discern what is true and good:

"Now, since everything chosen as a means is viewed as good or useful, and since good, as such, is the proper object of our desire, it follows that freedom of choice is a property of the will, or, rather, is identical with the will in so far as it has in its action the faculty of choice. But the will cannot proceed to act until it is enlightened by the knowledge possessed by the intellect. In other words, the good wished by the will is necessarily good in so far as it is known by the intellect; and this the more, because in all voluntary acts choice is subsequent to a judgment upon the truth of the good presented, declaring to which good preference should be given. No sensible man can doubt that judgment is an act of reason, not of the will. The end, or object, both of the rational will and of its liberty is that good only which is in conformity with reason."[118]

---

[116] *VS,* 86.

[117] *LP,* 5.

[118] *LP,* 5.

Thus, liberty must not be envisaged as an inborn capacity, but is more accurately described as an achieved and maintained *condition* which may exist to a greater or lesser degree in an individual depending on whether or not he lives within the dictates of right reason. "Such, then, being the condition of human liberty, it necessarily stands in need of light and strength to direct its actions to good and to restrain them from evil. Without this, the freedom of our will would be our ruin."[119]

c. Freedom and truth

What has been said so far can be summarized through words of Christ: "You will know the truth, and the truth will set you free."[120] For this reason he proclaimed to Pilate: "For this I was born, and for this I have come into the world, to bear witness to the truth."[121] And in bearing witness to truth, *he set humanity free.*

Thus, John Paul II spoke correctly when he said that the "[w]orship of God and a relationship with truth are revealed in Jesus Christ as the deepest foundation of freedom."[122] "[O]nly the freedom which submits to the Truth leads the human person to his true good. The good of the person is to be in the Truth and to *do* the Truth."[123]

d. Freedom and morality

Just as freedom is always dependent on the truth, it is also inescapably connected with the question of morality, since right conduct is nothing more than action in accordance with the truth. To illustrate this connection, John Paul II frames his discussion in *Veritatis Splendor* around Christ's conversation with the young rich man who asks: "Teacher, what good must I do to have eternal life?"[124] Based on this question and Christ's response to it, the saint explains:

---

[119] *LP,* 7.

[120] *Jn* 8:32.

[121] *Jn* 18:37.

[122] *VS,* 87.

[123] St. John Paul II, *Address to those taking part in the International Congress of Moral Theology* (April 10, 1986), 1.

"*The question of morality,* to which Christ provides the answer, *cannot prescind from the issue of freedom. Indeed, it considers that issue central,* for there can be no morality without freedom: 'It is only in freedom that man can turn to what is good'. *But what sort of freedom?* The Council, considering our contemporaries who 'highly regard' freedom and 'assiduously pursue' it, but who 'often cultivate it in wrong ways as a licence to do anything they please, even evil', speaks of *'genuine' freedom:* 'Genuine freedom is an outstanding manifestation of the divine image in man. For God willed to leave man 'in the power of his own counsel' (cf. *Sir* 15:14), so that he would seek his Creator of his own accord and would freely arrive at full and blessed perfection by cleaving to God'."[125]

Elsewhere the same pontiff explains that it was through the question of morality that God taught man to take his first steps in freedom. This was accomplished in the Garden of Eden by placing before man the tree of knowledge of good and evil.[126] The command "you shall not eat" is not some sort of cruel setup, a trap set for a creature doomed to failure: it was the necessary training ground for an education in freedom, the good of which was known to be so great that it was destined to outweigh any evil that might result from its abuse.[127]

It is through this example that we learn the positive purpose of moral prohibitions, and how "God's law does not reduce, much less do away with human freedom; rather, it protects and promotes that freedom."[128]

Here St. John Paul II is arguing against the popular tendency to speak of morality and freedom as if the two were in opposition, as if for one to

---

[124] *Mt* 19:16.

[125] *VS,* 34.

[126] St. John Paul II, *Theology of the Body* (Boston: 2006), pp. 150-156.

[127] *ST* I, q. 2, a. 3.

[128] *VS,* 25.

be cultivated the other must be destroyed. Leo XIII had dealt with the same misunderstanding long before him, and had spoken against it frequently in his battle with the Enlightenment philosophers: "Nothing more foolish can be uttered or conceived than the notion that, because man is free by nature, he is therefore exempt from law. Were this the case, it would follow that to become free we must be deprived of reason."[129] Moral laws, far from depriving the human being of his freedom, "make him at once the possessor of a more perfect liberty."[130]

> "Man's *genuine moral autonomy* in no way means the rejection but rather the acceptance of the moral law, of God's command: 'The Lord God gave this command to the man...' (*Gen2*:16). *Human freedom and God's law meet and are called to intersect,* in the sense of man's free obedience to God and of God's completely gratuitous benevolence towards man. Hence obedience to God is not, as some would believe, a *heteronomy,* as if the moral life were subject to the will of something all-powerful, absolute, ex-traneous to man and intolerant of his freedom."[131]

e. Freedom and society

If human freedom is brought to fruition to a greater or lesser extent depending on the degree to which the individual acts in conformity with truth and the will of God, then we can apply the same reasoning to society as a whole:

> "From this it is manifest that the eternal law of God is the sole standard and rule of human liberty, not only in each individual man, but also in the community and civil society which men constitute when united. Therefore, the true liberty of human society does not consist in every man doing what he pleases, for this would simply end in turmoil and confusion, and bring on the overthrow of the State; but rather in this, that through the

---

[129] *LP*, 7.
[130] *LP*, 12.
[131] *VS*, 41.

injunctions of the civil law all may more easily conform to the prescriptions of the eternal law."[132]

"Therefore, the nature of human liberty, however it be considered, whether in individuals or in society, whether in those who command or in those who obey, supposes the necessity of obedience to some supreme and eternal law, which is no other than the authority of God, commanding good and forbidding evil. And, so far from this most just authority of God over men diminishing, or even destroying their liberty, it protects and perfects it, for the real perfection of all creatures is found in the prosecution and attainment of their respective ends; but the supreme end to which human liberty must aspire is God."[133]

f. Freedom, natural law, and the body

Our discussion would not be complete if we failed to take into account the body as it pertains to freedom. In the eyes of natural law, the body acts as a fundamental part of morality and the exercise of freedom, but as freedom became doctrinaire, considered more and more in terms of liberal and libertarian ideologies, the body became irrelevant—a mere vehicle for use by the person trapped within it, a piece of property owned by the self, to be used according to whim and fancy, with nothing more to tell us about right conduct. This becomes blatantly obvious in systems where freedom is viewed as absolute, at which point the body is deprived of all objective meaning and is treated as chattel or property:

"A freedom which claims to be absolute ends up treating the human body as a raw datum, devoid of any meaning and moral values until freedom has shaped it in accordance with its design. Consequently, human nature and the body appear as *presuppositions or preambles,* materially *necessary* for freedom to make its choice, yet extrinsic to the person, the subject and the human act…This moral theory does

---

[132] *LP,* 10.
[133] *LP,* 11.

not correspond to the truth about man and his freedom. It contradicts the *Church's teachings on the unity of the human person,* whose rational soul is *per se et essentialiter* the form of his body. The spiritual and immortal soul is the principle of unity of the human being, whereby it exists as a whole — *corpore et anima unus* — as a person. These definitions not only point out that the body, which has been promised the resurrection, will also share in glory. They also remind us that reason and free will are linked with all the bodily and sense faculties."[134]

The body, because it has meaning, also has the ability to inform us as to the content of natural law, and as such it is never a hindrance but a created good, ready to assist man in the pursuit of the truth. Because of this it is an error to reduce morality to a spiritual and abstract thing, as if man were not both body *and* soul:

"*A doctrine which dissociates the moral act from the bodily dimensions of its exercise is contrary to the teaching of Scripture and Tradition.* Such a doctrine revives, in new forms, certain ancient errors which have always been opposed by the Church, inasmuch as they reduce the human person to a 'spiritual' and purely formal freedom. This reduction misunderstands the moral meaning of the body and of kinds of behaviour involving it...*body and soul are inseparable:* in the person, in the willing agent and in the deliberate act, *they stand or fall together.*"[135]

It is only through these precepts that the meaning of the natural law can be properly grasped:

"The natural moral law expresses and lays down the purposes, rights and duties which are based upon the bodily and spiritual nature of the human person. Therefore this law cannot be thought of as simply a set of norms on the biological level; rather it must be

---

[134] *VS,* 48.
[135] *VS,* 49.

defined as the rational order whereby man is called by the Creator to direct and regulate his life and actions and in particular to make use of his own body."[136]

The natural law does not allow for any division between freedom and nature, but rather acts as a harmonizing principle between the two.[137]

g. Freedom and conscience

We are now capable of addressing the issue of the relationship between conscience and freedom. This relationship is of particular importance in our present political context, where debates frequently erupt regarding what pertains to the private judgement of the individual's conscience, what behavior can be coerced by a social authority, and what authority is capable of decided on such things. These debates sooner or later lead to the invocation of phrases such as the "primacy of conscience," or complaints that a particular issue is a matter for "prudential judgment." These two concepts are distinct in themselves, but tend to become confused when converted into political slogans—but always they pertain to freedom and are invoked under the pretense of defending a valid freedom. We will discuss each of these at a later point, when we come to the subject of Catholic morality in particular,[138] but for now we should pause to mention that the conscience itself, while it must always be respected, can never be imagined as something operating arbitrarily, as if it has no limits or obligations external to itself. Its freedom must be considered in the same fashion as in the preceding sections. The proper view can be summarized in the words of John Paul II:

> "Although each individual has a right to be respected in his own journey in search of the truth, there exists a prior moral obligation, and a grave one at that, to seek the truth and to adhere to it once it is known. As Cardinal John Henry Newman, that outstanding

---

[136] *DV*, Introduction, 3.

[137] *VS*, 50.

[138] See section 4, parts 1c and 4g.

defender of the rights of conscience, forcefully put it: 'Conscience has rights because it has duties'."[139]

Although a lengthy discussion could be carried out with respect to what this means in practice for political and religious authorities, those points will be elaborated elsewhere. Here we will merely mention that the most important duty of the conscience is to be properly formed, and formed by that teacher who is most competent to instruct it, which is the Church:

> "...the authority of the Church, when she pronounces on moral questions, in no way undermines the freedom of conscience of Christians. This is so not only because freedom of conscience is never freedom 'from' the truth but always and only freedom 'in' the truth, but also because the Magisterium does not bring to the Christian conscience truths which are extraneous to it; rather it brings to light the truths which it ought already to possess, developing them from the starting point of the primordial act of faith. The Church puts herself always and only at the *service of conscience,* helping it to avoid being tossed to and fro by every wind of doctrine proposed by human deceit (cf. *Eph* 4:14), and helping it not to swerve from the truth about the good of man, but rather, especially in more difficult questions, to attain the truth with certainty and to abide in it."[140]

h. Slavery

It seems prudent to close our discussion of freedom with a few observations regarding slavery. This is because, as obvious as it may seem, the prevalent misunderstanding of human liberty leads directly to a misunderstanding of its opposite extreme. For example, because of the tendency to oversimplify freedom as the absence of restraints on personal conduct, then we inevitably reduce slavery to nothing more than an excessive restriction on one's actions. Usually once this

---

[139] *VS,* 34.
[140] *VS,* 64.

happens, the defenders of this misunderstood freedom begin to construe every limit to freedom as a step in the direction of slavery, which is obviously not the case at all.

However, if we take into consideration what has been said above, we see first and foremost that freedom consists in action in accordance with the true and the good, and that action in contradiction to truth and goodness is only the semblance of liberty. Thus, St. Thomas Aquinas, commenting on the words of our Lord, says the following:

> "Everything is that which belongs to it naturally. When, therefore, it acts through a power outside itself, it does not act of itself, but through another, that is, as a slave. But man is by nature rational. When, therefore, he acts according to reason, he acts of himself and according to his free will; and this is liberty. Whereas, when he sins, he acts in opposition to reason, is moved by another, and is the victim of foreign misapprehensions. Therefore, 'Whosoever committeth sin is the slave of sin.'"[141]

Leo XIII observed that even the pagans recognized this fact when they said that the wise man alone is free.[142]

Yet our study would be incomplete if we did not mention a second aspect of the Christian doctrine concerning slavery, which perhaps runs even more contrary to the modern way of thinking. Because freedom is often seen as an absolute good, then it is easy to draw the conclusion, unconsciously and automatically, that any sort of servitude is somehow subhuman and evil. But scripture and the constant teachings of the Church again offer a much different view. Since liberty lies in conformity with the good, then it is more accurate to say that slavery is only degrading to the person if he is enslaved to sin; but, on the contrary, slavery to God would amount to the highest realization of liberty.

---

[141] St. Thomas Aquinas, *On the Gospel of St. John*, ch. 8, lect. 4, n. 3.
[142] *LP*, 6.

And so we conclude with words of warning given by St. Augustine:

> "In the house of the Lord, slavery is free. It is free because it serves not out of necessity, but out of charity... Charity should make you a servant, just as truth has made you free... you are at once both a servant and free: a servant, because you have become such; free, because you are loved by God your Creator; indeed, you have also been enabled to love your Creator... You are a servant of the Lord and you are a freedman of the Lord. Do not go looking for a liberation which will lead you far from the house of your liberator!"[143]

7. Justice

Justice is briefly defined as "the constant and firm will to give their due to God and neighbor."[144] In more familiar terms, it is the precept that we must treat every other person as if they were persons, and not as if they were objects or pieces of furniture. It concerns our attitude and action not only toward individuals, but toward our community and other communities, and vice versa. It is, according to the *Compendium*, the "decisive criteria of morality" in the social sphere.[145] But so far we have only spoken generally and vaguely, and this will not help us when it comes to application and action. Therefore we must dig a bit further into the problem of justice, and consider it in the traditional fashion, as divided into four parts: commutative, distributive, legal, and social. Because justice is an intrinsically relational principle, it is divided into parts depending on the nature of the relationship in question.[146]

a. Commutative Justice

The first and most immediately apparent economic relationship is that which exists between one individual and another in daily commerce. Because this sort of justice concerns contracts between individuals and

---

[143] St. Augustine, *Enarratio in Psalmum XCIX*, 7.
[144] *CCC*, 1807.
[145] *CSDC*, 201.
[146] See also: *ST* II-II, q. 61, a. 1; *CCC*, 2426; *CSDC*, 201; *CV*, 36-37.

strictly follows the principle of "equality in exchange," we call this justice *commutative*. Commutative justice obliges that we pay others what we owe them, fulfilling our contractual obligations to the greatest extent possible. [147]

b. Distributive Justice

Next we come to the relationship between the community at large and the individual. When we consider this relationship from the point of view of the community, it is called *distributive* justice, as opposed to *legal justice*, which is the same relationship viewed from the other direction—from the point of view of the individual. Distributive justice regulates those things owed by the community to a participating and law-abiding member according to his contribution and need.[148] It is in accordance with distributive justice that governing officials must judge whether or not a market is operating to the benefit of each individual in a just manner, and if this is not the case then it may be legitimate to pursue justice through adjustments to market structures, as well as through mechanisms of redistribution.[149]

c. Legal justice

Also called "contributive justice," legal justice concerns the relationship between the individual and the community at large. Considered as such, it is the same relationship as that of distributive justice, only from the opposite point of view. It directs an individual as to what he owes the society in which he lives. The obligation to pay taxes to a government authority in order to contribute to the common good is an example of legal justice.[150]

---

[147] *CCC*, 2411.

[148] *ST* II-II, q. 61, aa. 1-2.

[149] As abhorrent as the very word "redistribution" has become in certain circles, Benedict XVI invoked it no less than eight times in *Caritas in Veritate* (see paragraphs 32, 36, 37, 39, 42, 49).

[150] *CCC*, 2411.

d. Social Justice

Last, we may speak of the most general concept of justice, which is for that reason called *social*. Because of its nature, this form of justice circumscribes everything else—ordering, subordinating, but never eliminating or destroying, the other forms.[151] This point of view addresses structural problems and formulates appropriate solutions at a broad level.

e. Ideology and the oversimplification of justice

Having delineated the various *types* of justice, all of which must be taken into consideration when discussing CST, we can now see that, historically speaking, the greatest offenses against justice do not come from a total rejection of justice, but rather from an emphasis on one part of justice to the exclusion of certain others. To say the same thing another way, the problem of justice has historically been one of partiality and oversimplification. This is most evident when examining the history of ideologies, which are by definition oversimplifications of reality in an attempt to solve large problems with sweeping generalizations. Capitalist ideology, for example, has a history of insisting on the importance of commutative justice (justice in exchange) while disregarding or denying validity of distributive justice.[152] Socialism, on the other hand, gives an almost exclusive emphasis to distributive justice, and consequently neglects the role of commutative justice. Capitalism and Socialism, both being market ideologies, reveal the problems inherent in naïve and simplistic worldviews which try to address all social problems in terms of just one kind of justice. This is also why the Church so often adopts the point of view of social justice: this is not because she prefers one justice to another, but because social justice involves the broadest possible view of the economic field, and is therefore capable of taking into account and ordering the other parts within it so that they can work in harmony with one another.

---

[151] *CCC*, 2426; *CSDC*, 201.
[152] *CV*, 35.

Section IV. Morality

The social doctrine of the Church presupposes its moral foundations. For this reason, although it is possible to discuss social doctrine without making mention of the moral philosophy which acts as its substructure, it is good practice not to pass over it in silence. This is, first of all, because there are aspects of the moral teachings of the Church which are foreign even to many Catholics; and, second, because even those to whom the teachings are familiar will find a review helpful in light of the present study.

1. Natural Law

a. Which law? What nature?

Whenever someone mentions "natural law" there is an immediate confusion that usually arises due to the contemporary understanding of the word "nature." In modern usage we associate the terms "nature" and "natural" with the "natural world," which is to say, the universal laws of physics and biology and all of the mechanisms that take place on this level. We don't attribute to the word "nature" anything specifically human. It is taken as a context for all life rather than as a distinctive characteristic of a given being.

But when the Church speaks of "nature," and especially when it speaks of natural law, it is speaking very differently. This is because natural law teaches that every being has its own "nature," and that this imbedded nature also corresponds to an imbedded "natural law" which tends the being toward the perfection of its specific nature. It follows then that the "nature" in question will always be different depending on whether we are talking about a vegetable, an animal, or the human person. What is according to the "natural law" for one category of beings may not apply to another, because they have different natures. This is why the tendency to imagine "nature" as mere biological necessity applying to all material beings *in the same way* is a drastic oversimplification. Rather, when we are concerned with human behavior, we are concerned with man's specific nature and, more importantly, his last end toward which this nature tends to move.

For example, we might say that sexual desire is "natural." If we make the mistake of taking "natural law" to mean "biological necessity," then we might end up drawing the conclusion that promiscuous sex is according to the natural law, since we see it all the time in animals and in fact this behavior is necessary to many of them. But we cannot transpose this principle onto a different nature—for example, onto human nature. Sexual desire is still in accordance with natural law for human nature, but only insofar as it reinforces the being's development toward its ultimate perfection. While for certain animal natures this entails promiscuous sex, for man it does not. Sexual desire is therefore "natural" to man in a very different way than it is "natural" to animals, because man has different faculties and a different perfection which he must realize. He *has a different nature* and so the natural law does not direct him in the same way as it would direct a vegetable; likewise, the vegetable is directed very differently than a fish or a bird.

In order to gain a proper perspective on this subject, we must return to a more comprehensive notion of law capable of taking into account a hierarchy of orders and contexts, and which can deal with the diversity of life we find in the world. In traditional terminology, we must return to the three orders of law: eternal, natural, human.

b. Eternal law

Whenever we come upon a community of beings ruled by a sovereign who directs them toward their good, we come upon a law. If there are different kinds of these communities, they will be directed by a different kind of law. Now, the first and foremost of communities is the universe. The universe and every being within it are sustained in their very existence by the will of God and act in accordance with his rule. From this single rule, which is called *eternal law*, all other varieties of law are derived.[153]

---

[153] *ST*I-II, q. 91, a. 1; *ST*I-II, q. 93, aa. 1-6.

c. Natural law

In every created thing there is an inclination, impressed upon the very substance of the creature, drawing it toward certain ends. These ends are the mark of what the *eternal law* demands of that specific nature. It follows logically that this law will be different for each nature, depending on the *end* toward which the eternal law directs it. Man, for example, has divine beatitude for his end, whereas animals and vegetable life do not. And so, the inclinations of each will vary. When we obey this law which is "written on our natures,"[154] we obey the law of our nature—our *natural law*. Because this natural law is really just the eternal as it pertains to us as men, then it is true that when we obey it we are participating in the eternal law. This is why it is said that the natural law is derived from and never contradicts the eternal law.[155]

d. Human law

Why then, if there is a natural law written in the hearts of men, do we not find the same laws and customs in every society? Why, if all men possess the same nature and therefore the same natural law, does every society have different laws? The explanation for this lies in the third kind of law, which is called *human law*. The difference between natural law and human law is that natural law provides general precepts which are everywhere the same, while human law represents particular applications of these precepts. Because every nation and historical period differs and therefore has different needs, its *applications* of the precepts will be incredibly diverse, even though the precepts themselves will remain the same. This is a valid diversity so long as they accord with natural law and, through this, eternal law. It is only by ultimately deriving from the eternal law that any lower form of law has its validity:

> "Human law is law only by virtue of its accordance with right reason; and thus it is manifest that it flows from the eternal law.

---

[154] *ST* I-II, q. 94, a. 6.
[155] *ST* I-II, q. 91, a. 2.

And in so far as it deviates from right reason it is called an unjust law; in such case it is no law at all, but rather a species of violence."[156]

e. The precepts of the natural law

In order to understand why human law is diverse while natural law is said to be everywhere the same, we must remember that, much like how the Church offers principles rather than technical solutions, the natural law offers *precepts* rather than applications. And the first precept of the natural law is simply this: *good is to be sought and evil avoided.*[157]

Further precepts are dictated by man's nature: he is a being, he is a living being, and he is a rational being. Corresponding to these three facts about man's nature are three natural precepts: first, man must conserve his being, which we call the duty of "self-preservation"; further, he must reproduce himself, raise his children, etc.; and last, which is specific to man as a rational being, he is to actively seek what is good. It is only due to this last feature that man can be considered "responsible" for his decisions. Animals, being irrational and therefore unable to rationally seek conformity with the natural law, follow it automatically and without their conscious assent. Only man can consciously participate in, or revolt against, the natural law.

From these observations we can begin to see why human law is diverse. Although the precepts are everywhere the same, we should expect that, depending on time and place, people will find various means of fulfilling these precepts. Also, because some of these men will make better use of their rational faculties, the various human laws will be more or less in conformity to the natural law. All will not be equal, although all can be said to be striving after the same justice.

f. Not everything in nature is natural

---

[156] *ST* I-II, q. 93, a. 3.
[157] *ST* I-II, q. 94, a. 2.

One further confusion needs to be set aright, if only because it is so common. Consider the following statement: "Whatever exists, is found in nature, and is therefore natural." This way of thinking—called "naturalism"—leads to the rejection of any morality whatsoever, because it rejects the possibility of anything being unnatural. But we must recall that the Church does not speak of "nature" simply in terms of "everything that exists." Certainly the Church acknowledges the totality of creation as "nature," but it considers it as a grand diversity and within the context of natural law, which takes into account the particular *end* toward which a being tends. Considered in this way, if an action or behavior conforms with its proper end (or its "perfection"),[158] then and only then is it natural. Thus, we can easily imagine acts which are in no way ordained to the proper end of the nature in question. For example, the sexual function and the pleasure associated with it are natural insofar as they conform to their obvious natural ends; they are unnatural when they do not. The deviant who seeks pleasure with himself alone short-circuits both the purpose of the sexual function and the pleasure associated with it. An analogous consideration can be found in the intellectual sphere: although human reasoning is performed by the "rational faculty," no one would be naïve enough to claim that every decision produced by this faculty is therefore rational. Whether or not a decision is rational depends not on whether or not it is produced through the rational faculty, but whether or not it was produced in conformity with the laws proper to that sphere. It is entirely possible for the rational faculty to produce irrational conclusions. Returning now to the sphere of natural law, we must not lose our ability to distinguish the normal ("natural") from the pathological ("unnatural"), simply because they both appear "in nature."

2. Conscience

CST has been described as *the intersection between the Christian conscience and the real world*.[159] This is an interesting way of speaking: it points out the truth that conscience is not determined wholly by

---

158 *ST* I-II, q. 94, a. 2.
159 *CSDC*, 73.

worldly conditions, but at the same time that it ought to be connected to these conditions in some fashion. This connection, which forms the conscience with respect to real life conditions, is represented by CST. We are therefore justified in pausing to elaborate on the proper notion of the conscience, although this may appear at first to be an unnecessary digression.

a. What is a "good conscience"?

It has been a constant teaching of the Catholic Church that individuals are bound to obey the judgment of their conscience, and that to disobey this guide is to condemn oneself. Such a stance, however, is easily misconstrued, for it must be understood within the context of the entire Catholic truth about the conscience, its formation, and its exercise.

The degree to which the teaching has in fact been misconstrued is evident by the common phrase: "in good conscience." When a person says this, they usually mean to imply that they acted in accordance with their conscience when they made the decision. Unfortunately, putting things this way is really to skip a step. Just because a person may act according to his or her conscience does not mean that the conscience was "good." It simply means that they obeyed it. It is possible to have a "bad" conscience and to obey *that*.

What this means is that we have two things to consider when it comes to the conscience. First we must ensure that our conscience is healthy. That is to say we must take great care to have formed a "good conscience." This will not just happen automatically. Second, and only after we have accomplished the first task, we must follow the judgement of the conscience. This is a very important point to emphasize, because it is conceivable that a situation could arise in which it is unwise to trust too easily one's own conscience. A man given to drug addiction or habituated to pornography may very well engage in these activities "in good conscience," meaning that his conscience is not disturbed by participating in them. Such is a case of a de-formed conscience, and such a man would do better to trust an upright neighbor. Too often, and no doubt under the influence of a certain humanistic naivety which assumes that the conscience is always good, we neglect the first step—the duty to "train" one's conscience—and think only of the second. We end by obeying an ill-formed conscience, and in such cases where the deformation is due to our own laxity or negligence, we will rightly be held responsible for the error.

b. Conscience is not infallible

The error mentioned above, which causes us to follow the dictates of our conscience without also taking steps to ensure that our conscience is properly formed, is a recipe for disaster. It treats as infallible the inner light which, although naturally disposed toward the good, is not invincibly oriented toward it, and which can become atrophied, darkened, or distorted through personal neglect.

c. The problem with 'primacy of conscience'

With the phrase "primacy of conscience," we encounter the same problem we did when discussing prudence, and we have thought it wise to dwell on it for the same reason: because it is an error so common that it has become almost a popular slogan.

We must consider an imaginary case, which is found far too often in actual experience. Let's say a man's conscience nudges him in a certain direction on the issue of abortion. If this is honestly the case, is it valid for him to go against the Church's constant teaching on the matter, claiming "primacy of conscience?" It depends: is his conscience well-formed? Has he taken the trouble to educate himself and to hear the arguments which underlie the Church's position? If he has not, then it is possible he is not exercising his conscience at all, but is merely exercising his preference. Or, to say the same thing another way: one's conscience is never formed in a vacuum, and because of this, and due to individual negligence, it may well be "misinformed," or formed in the image of our own arbitrary desires.

The point is not to invalidate the concept of "primacy of conscience," which is one of the most noble teachings of the Catholic Tradition. But we must always keep in mind that the claim to "primacy of conscience" presupposes a constant effort to form one's conscience, in the same way that the claim to "prudential judgment" presupposes the constant development of prudence. In both cases, laying claim to the right requires a great deal of practice and discipline. Without this discipline, both "primacy of conscience" or "prudential judgement" are simply not possible, and to claim them amounts to nothing more than escapism.

3. Act and intention

a. Subjective morality

The problems of conscience we have mentioned above, and the moral incoherence that results from a misunderstanding of its nature, tend toward what can be called "subjective morality." Earlier we mentioned the danger of considering the physical world as secondary or "less real," and imagining the "inner life" as what "really matters," particularly when it comes to the determination of right and wrong. This tendency toward subjectivity finds little to check it in the modern mentality of abstraction, and it inevitably leads to the dangerous notion that, because a person *intended* good to come from his actions, then these actions are automatically rendered moral, or, at worst, pre-moral. Even if these actions have been judged by the Church as "intrinsically evil," some would claim that, so long as there was a "good intention," then the individual cannot be considered morally culpable. Such a way of thinking seems reasonable at first glance, but it amounts to the denial of any objective rule by which actions can be judged. It becomes entirely subjective, and this subjective morality ends by severing the connection between body and soul, conscience and concrete reality.

To remedy this problem, the Church continuously insists that the *"morality of the human act depends primarily and fundamentally on the 'object' rationally chosen by the deliberate will,"*[160] meaning that it is the object (the concrete act) and not the subject (the person acting) by which the rightness of the act is to be judged. The object is the not the far-removed end that the person had in mind—their "motivation"—but

---

[160] *VS*, 78.

is the concrete act itself. In other words, *the end cannot justify the means*. Thus, the goodness of an act is objectively determinable without reference to one's intention.

b. Doing evil that good may come of it

The great danger of this sort of thinking was condemned long ago by St. Paul (Romans 3:8), and was long after summarized by Pope Paul IV:

> "Though it is true that sometimes it is lawful to tolerate a lesser moral evil in order to avoid a greater evil or in order to promote a greater good, it is never lawful, even for the gravest reasons, to do evil that good may come of it (cf. *Rom* 3:8) — in other words, to intend directly something which of its very nature contradicts the moral order, and which must therefore be judged unworthy of man, even though the intention is to protect or promote the welfare of an individual, of a family or of society in general."[161]

The principle is simple: *it is never permissible to do evil so that good may come of it.* "The greater good"—a common justification for acts such as abortion, torture, etc., is never a valid excuse for the choice of intrinsically evil acts, because the act in each case—the "object" rationally chosen by the will—is in itself evil. As noble and free as the human will might be, it cannot change an evil act into a righteous one simply by having good intentions, any more than a good intention can turn vinegar into wine. Each act must conform to the good.

4. The exercise of prudence

Just as the phrase "primacy of conscience" is easily politicized into a meaningless slogan, so also the concept of "prudential judgement" is often thrown about in such a way that becomes nothing more than an excuse used to justify any type of action or ideology that an individual prefers. But prudence, like conscience, requires progressive formation, and the individual who neglects this preliminary step is not justified in defending his decisions by saying he is acting according to *prudence*. To

---

[161] *HV,* 14.

understand what is meant by "preliminary formation," we can refer once more to St. Thomas, who considered the virtue of prudence to have eight parts: memory, understanding, docility, diligence, reason, foresight, circumspection, and caution.[162] However, after the fashion of the *Compendium* and for the sake of clarity, we will describe the five most prominent parts here. The interested reader can refer to the relevant articles of the *Summa* for an elaboration of all eight.[163]

a. Memory

Memory is the first of three "cognitive dispositions" which permit the development of the necessary conditions for the actual exercise of prudence, and without which the exercise of prudential judgment is only an illusion. The healthy disposition of memory is bound to assist in the effective exercise of prudence because it gives he who develops it the capacity to recall and reflect upon past experiences in an objective fashion, and without falsification.[164]

b. Docility

Second of the cognitive dispositions is *docility*, which allows one to learn from others and to profit from their experience on the basis of an authentic love for truth.[165] It is therefore closely linked with humility, and is a mode of its expression. Christ told his apostles that "He who hears you, hears me."[166] Without a carefully developed sense of docility, we run the risk of remaining deaf to the apostles' exhortations, preferring instead our own opinions and prejudices.[167]

c. Diligence

Diligence is the third of the cognitive dispositions. Diligence concerns the ability to face the unexpected with objectivity in order to turn every

---

[162] *ST* II-II, q. 48.
[163] *ST* II-II, qq. 48-49.
[164] *ST* II-II, q. 49, a. 1.
[165] *ST* II-II, q. 49, a. 3.
[166] *Lk* 10:16.
[167] *CCC,* 87.

situation to the service of good, overcoming the temptation of intemperance, injustice, and cowardice.[168]

d. Foresight

The three dispositions just mentioned *prepare the way* for prudence to be exercised effectively in the concrete moment of decision. Within the moment of decision itself—which has been called *prudence as commanding*—there are two we must consider, which concern the future and the past in relation to the present. Foresight is the first of these, and is the capacity to weigh the efficacy of a given conduct for the attainment of a moral end.[169]

e. Circumspection

Second, concerning the past, we come to circumspection, which is the capacity to weigh the circumstances that contributed to the creation of the situation in which a given action will be carried out.[170]

f. Participation and Obedience

Having examined some of the parts of prudence, we must now consider prudence in the social context. Here the exercise of prudence appears in two forms—*active prudence* and *passive prudence*. The first is an expression of our responsibility to participate in the ordering of society toward the good, and the second involves the obedience and submission each of us owes to the social authority, so long as this submission does not compromise human dignity.[171] It should not come as a surprise to us that in individualistic and rationalistic ages the second form—obedience—is often ignored or rejected outright, but both kinds of prudence are necessary in order to achieve a complete picture of our subject. The man who knows how to act but not how to listen, learn, and obey, is at best half prudent.

---

[168] *ST* II-II, q. 49, a. 4.
[169] *ST* II-II, q. 49, a. 6.
[170] *ST* II-II, q. 49, a. 7.
[171] *ST* II-II, q. 50, aa. 1-2.

g. The problem with 'prudential judgment'

Now we may refer again to what was said at the beginning of this section. It should be clear now that there is more to the exercise of prudence than the simple claim that "I have considered the matter and I am doing what I think is best." Quite often we hear sincere believers adopting this stance in order to disregard or oppose the teachings of a pope, taking refuge in this supposed "prudential judgment," believing that by doing so they escape any sort of guilt for their departure from the Magisterium. But if such a person has not been carefully cultivating and forming the virtue of prudence, then it should be clear that prudential judgment is a simple impossibility. Far from being a "privilege" that one is born with and which one may invoke at any time, prudential judgment is rather a weighty undertaking that we find before us. Few ever become adequate to the task.

Now, as was the case with "primacy of conscience," we do not mean to disregard the possibility of prudential judgment as a valid concept: it is certainly possible that a particular papal suggestion or idea is not binding, or that a principle of CST is up for various forms of application depending on the situation. Applications do indeed call for prudential judgment. But, in actual experience, we find that the invocation of the phrase in question is rarely used within this legitimate context, and is more often a cop-out used to keep the Church from interfering with our political agendas.

5. Ignorance

Intimately connected to the question of prudence, its cultivation, and its exercise, as well as to the earlier questions of conscience and freedom, is the problem of ignorance, for ignorance is destructive of all three.

If we are called to freedom, then we are first and foremost called to know the truth: "Ye shall know the truth, and the truth shall set you free."[172] We are given no reason to believe that freedom can exist apart

---

[172] *Jn* 8:32.

from this truth. Therefore, to the degree that we lack the truth—which is to say, to the degree that we live in ignorance—we are not really free. Because of this, we can say that it is our responsibility to minimize and dispel ignorance whenever we can. We can also infer that we will be held responsible when our ignorance is of the sort that could have easily been dispelled but which, for whatever reason, we allowed to persist.[173]

a. Two kinds of ignorance

Although ignorance is undesirable, it is also unavoidable, as our mental capacities are finite. However, since it is obvious from what has been said above that, to some extent, we are responsible for our ignorance, then we arrive at a twofold division of ignorance: the first is known as *invincible* ignorance, and this is the kind of ignorance for which we are not morally responsible. The second is called *vincible* ignorance because it refers to a condition of ignorance which could have been removed if only the individual had taken the proper steps to remove it. Further comment on each of these is necessary in order to flesh out the distinction.

b. Invincible ignorance

We are all of us born ignorant of just about everything, and even if we live diligently we will still have a lot to learn by the time we die. The natural consequence of this inevitable state of ignorance is that we will constantly make mistakes due to our lack of knowledge of the truth. In fact, it might be legitimate to say that man in general, insofar as he is fallen, is more often separated from God due to ignorance than to evil plain and simple, and that the sins a man commits are more often the result of wrong-headedness than hard-heartedness. According to Pope Leo XIII:

"It is rather ignorance than ill-will which keeps multitudes away from Jesus Christ. There are many who study humanity and the natural world; few who study the Son of God. The first step, then, is

---

[173] *VS*, 62.

to substitute knowledge for ignorance, so that He may no longer be despised or rejected because He is unknown."[174]

Observing this, and considering the fact that a man cannot be held responsible for a sin in which his will gave no real assent, we can say that this inevitable, invincible sort of ignorance is not a sin. However, there is an underlying assumption that goes along with this notion of invincible ignorance, which is that we have at the same time *done our best* to overcome it and minimize its impact on our lives.

c. Vincible ignorance

Now we must look at the other side of the picture. When a person "takes little trouble to find out what is true and good, or when conscience is almost blinded through the habit of committing sin,"[175] then we can hardly say that his ignorance (and whatever actions stem from it) are "inevitable." In these cases we must admit that due to his own choices (mental sloth or habitual sin) his ignorance is *vincible* and that he is to some degree responsible for it. In short, he could have had the light, but chose the darkness instead. This means that if we are too lazy to educate our conscience and participate in its formation, it will naturally become deformed, and this state of things will be our own fault. Likewise, if we allow ourselves to live in constant sin, our consciences will be desensitized and our judgment thrown askew. In such circumstances, we are clearly responsible for our negligence.[176]

6. Specific issues and applications

The following sections are intended to provide the reader with more specific examples of how the Church deals with moral issues. The list is obviously not exhaustive, nor can it be said to include even the most important moral questions that are today under discussion. The items included have been chosen simply due to their familiarity to the

---

[174] *TFP*, 13.
[175] *GS*, 16.
[176] *CCC*, 1790-1791.

contemporary audience, and because they illustrate well the application of the principles outlined above.

a. Lying

According to St. Augustine: "A lie consists in speaking a falsehood with the intention of deceiving."[177] Such an act is the most direct offense against truth, because it destroys another man's relation to it, as well as destroying the relation between the liar and the one being lied to,[178] undermining the purpose of communication itself.

The example of the lie, because it is identified as intrinsically evil,[179] offers an excellent case point with regard to the error of *consequentialism* mentioned above, which would have us believe that there is such a thing as a "white lie"—a lie that is permissible because it does little or no harm. Even worse, the consequentialist would suggest that it is in fact *necessary* to lie in great matters, provided that some good result is to come from the dishonesty. Here the adherents of consequentialist thinking will automatically formulate the most extreme examples to prove their point: "What if I were hiding Jews during the Holocaust and Nazi soldiers came to my door? Are you really saying that I should give up the innocent in order to avoid lying?"

It is a tragic situation, to be sure, but if the protection of the bodily safety of the innocent were a reasonable cause to abandon the truth, then all the deaths of the martyrs in Christian history are worthy more of ridicule than of respect. All of the martyrs chose a violent end rather than deny the truth in which they believed, and are senseless from the point of view of consequentialism. To further clarify a situation such as that mentioned above, we must remember that a person may withhold information from those who do not have a right to know,[180] but it is *never permissible to tell a falsehood*. Discretion is appropriate,

---

[177] St. Augustine, *De mendacio* 4, 5.
[178] *CCC,* 2483.
[179] *CCC,* 2485.
[180] *CCC,* 2488-9.

especially in the use of language, but never a lie, for as always "we may not do evil that good may come of it."[181]

b. Abortion

Abortion is another intrinsically evil act[182] that is, nonetheless, frequently defended on the grounds that to commit it in certain situations in necessary and therefore permissible. But the Church has always insisted that human life retains its dignity, regardless of whether or not it is too young or too old to defend this dignity for itself. This is why abortion and euthanasia are often condemned in the same sentence, because both acts prey upon life in its extremes: "the direct interruption of the generative process already begun and, above all, all direct abortion, even for therapeutic reasons, are to be absolutely excluded as lawful means of regulating the number of children."[183]

Here again, as a reminder and in order to refute those who choose to absolutize the rights of man, it needs to be said that "[j]ust as man does not have unlimited dominion over his body in general, so also, and with more particular reason, he has no such dominion over his specifically sexual faculties, for these are concerned by their very nature with the generation of life, of which God is the source."[184] One does not "own" his or her own body, much less is permissible to deal violently with a human life nourished within it.

And so John XXIII remind us: "Human life is sacred—all men must recognize that fact. From its very inception it reveals the creating hand of God."[185]

c. Homosexuality

If we wish to illustrate the connection between Catholic morality and natural law, then sexual deviation is an appropriate subject for analysis.

---

[181] *CCC,* 1756; *VS,* 79-83.
[182] *VS,* 80.
[183] *HV,* 14.
[184] *HV,* 13.
[185] *MM,* 194.

We said earlier that the mere fact that a behavior is found in nature does not make it *natural*. Likewise, pleasures which are contrary to nature so far as a species is concerned can seem "natural" to individuals—but this does not mean the pleasure is natural. It may be pathological. An individual with an inverted sexual attraction will be attracted to members of his own sex; it is natural, in this sense, for an invert to conduct himself as such, but this does not make inversion normal. While a man may seek pleasure with other men, it is opposed to nature that he engage in such a sterile union. The pleasures associated with homosexuality are *in* nature, but are at the same time *opposed* to nature.

Now it should be said that, even if an individual's idiosyncrasies relegate him to the margin of his species in such a way, he is not necessarily condemned thereby, as we shall see in the next section. As Etienne Gilson so ably put it: "Moral science alone is not enough either to condemn men or absolve them, but it does suffice to distinguish good from evil, and it sees to it that vice is not exalted into virtue."[186]

d. Torture

Once we have acknowledged that evil may not be done for the sake of any greater good, many contemporary debates evaporate immediately. Arguments for abortion and dishonesty were two such instances—arguments in favor of torture are a third. Torture is constantly defended in the public sphere, usually on the basis of fantastic scenarios of cataclysmic proportions, in which a "ticking time bomb" is about to wreak havoc on a civilian population, and only the application of torture to a captive is likely to reveal its location.

Now at this point we could summon the testimony of any number of experts in the field, as well as historical examples, all of which would confirm for us that torture is simply not effective, regardless of the good press some circles would give it. But we need not engage in such

---

[186] Etienne Gilson, *The Christian Philosophy of St. Thomas Aquinas* (Notre Dame, 1994), p. 281.

research here because even if torture were proven effective—which we must not grant—it would still be illicit and intrinsically evil[187] by the fact that it rejects the dignity due to the person, a dignity which cannot be surrendered by the person and which does not depend on any action on their part.[188] The use of methods such as torture to coerce the will *treats the human being as a means rather than an end*, which the Church unfailingly rejects as a permissible attitude.[189]

e. Homicide

To take someone's life is the greatest of all thefts, for in stealing this one thing, everything else is stolen along with it. There are, in specific circumstances, justifiable killings, but these are carried out by a legitimate authority. The reason this is licit is due to the hierarchical nature of social authority.

For a plant to be sacrificed to the animal, and the animal to the man, is not out of the normal hierarchy of life. However, two men who are hierarchically each other's peers have no right to take such action. Thus, when it comes to the just extinction of a human life, we must turn to a superior authority, which in this case is the political authority. A properly constituted political authority is superior to the individual members of the social body from the standpoint of justice, and so the decision that one life must be removed from the whole can be justly made by that authority alone.[190]

Although the above reasoning legitimates the death penalty in theory, it must be remembered that even when a legitimate social authority exists, due to the intrinsic value of human life the death penalty should only be employed in cases of necessity, when society has no other means to protect itself from the menace of the criminal:

---

[187] *VS*, 80.
[188] *VS*, 90, 92.
[189] *VS*, 48.
[190] *ST* II-II, q. 64, aa. 2-3; *ST* II-II, q. 65, a. 1.

"It is clear that, for the [purposes of punishment] to be achieved, *the nature and extent of the punishment* must be carefully evaluated and decided upon, and [the state] ought not go to the extreme of executing the offender except in cases of absolute necessity: in other words, when it would not be possible otherwise to defend society. Today however, as a result of steady improvements in the organization of the penal system, such cases are very rare, if not practically non-existent."[191]

f. Suicide

Suicide is homicide against oneself, for one is bound to respect his own life in the same way as he is bound to respect the lives of others. And in fact, in the opinion of Aquinas, it is more grievous to kill oneself than another, because it is to oneself that one owes the greatest love.[192] Hence the command to *love our neigbors as ourselves.*

Here again we return to the misunderstandings caused by considering oneself as one's own "private property." If this were the case, then it would be easy to understand why killing another would be forbidden, since that would involve destruction of someone else's "private property"; unfortunately it would make it impossible to explain why killing oneself is at the same time unacceptable, since one may dispose of one's own property at will. To understand the evil of suicide we must abandon the idea of "self-ownership."

The evil of suicide is fundamentally linked with the evil of homicide, because it is violence against the dignity due to persons as persons. One's own life is not his own property to discard or do away with as he sees fit, any more than the life of anyone else, and to kill oneself is forbidden for the same reasons as homicide.[193]

---

[191] *EV*, 56. This passage also cited in the *Catechism.*
[192] *ST* II-II, q. 26, a. 4: "...out of charity, a man ought to love himself more than his neighbor."
[193] *ST,* II-II, q. 64, a. 5.

Further, there is also a social aspect to the problem: every man, as a member of society, has duties to that society, and the society has a right to his services. By killing himself he deprives the other members of society the good he was called to contribute.[194]

7. The question of culpability

Now after what has been said so far regarding morality, we must close by recalling that the Church refuses to "put God in a box." She allows Him the ability to grant mercy where He will, and at the same time acknowledges that, although there is an objective rule to right conduct, the question of *culpability* can and does vary depending on external circumstances and the inner state of the individual.

What this means is that although the Church is unfaltering in defending the reality of intrinsically evil acts, it does not pretend to know with precision exactly what degree of consent was present in the heart of the acting subject. The Church allows for the possibility that a person under extreme emotional duress, for example, cannot be held fully accountable for some acts. The acts remain evil from an objective standpoint, but depending on the degree of consent of the will of the individual, their culpability varies—and the ultimate judge of that culpability is God. Adopting the words of St. Lucy, we affirm that "without consent of the mind there is no stain on the body."[195] That is to say, he who does not consent with his will, does not sin, even if he engages in an intrinsically evil act.

---

[194] *In V Eth.,* 17.
[195] *ST* II-II, q. 65, a. 5.

Section V. Economic Life

Having laid the foundations for our study by examining the role of the Church,[196] the nature of man,[197] the rule of his conduct,[198] and the principles of Catholic Social Teaching in general,[199] we can now concern ourselves with the concrete application of all of these ideas within the economic sphere.

1. Four phases of economic activity

The first thing to be said about the Catholic view of economic activity is that it is not nearly as simple as those of contemporary ideological systems. Reality is not only complex, but also subtle. The Church, for example, stresses justice not only in a superficial and immediate sense, but in *every phase* of economic activity:

> "The Church's social doctrine has always maintained that *justice must be applied to every phase of economic activity*, because this is always concerned with man and his needs. Locating resources, financing, production, consumption and all the other phases in the economic cycle inevitably have moral implications. *Thus every economic decision has a moral consequence*. The social sciences and the direction taken by the contemporary economy point to the same conclusion. Perhaps at one time it was conceivable that first the creation of wealth could be entrusted to the economy, and then the task of distributing it could be assigned to politics. Today that would be more difficult, given that economic activity is no longer circumscribed within territorial limits, while the authority of governments continues to be principally local. Hence the canons of justice must be respected from the outset, as the economic process unfolds, and not just afterwards or incidentally."[200]

---

[196] See section I.
[197] See section II.
[198] See section IV.
[199] See section III.
[200] *CV*, 37.

This notion of "phases" is somewhat foreign to the modern economic outlook, although it was prevalent in the traditional ideas about political economy. According to the tradition of the Church from St. Augustine to St. Thomas, there are four distinct phases which must be taken into account. These are *production*, *exchange*, *distribution*, and *consumption*.

One of the unique obsessions of modernity is its mania for oversimplification.[201] Everything must be reduced to its most basic form. As could be easily guessed, subtlety does not fare well as this tendency progresses. With Adam Smith and the birth of modern economic theory the older and more comprehensive theory was pared down to production and exchange alone (and even these were retained only in an impoverished form). Eventually a form of the third element, distribution, was re-added by the "neoclassical" economists, but no one has been willing to rediscover the fourth and most important piece—which is the actual consumption of the goods—and so these approaches are deficient.

2. The three false commodities—land, labor, money

Modernity's oversimplification mania always ends by ignoring vital distinctions. Sweeping generalizations are made, and things themselves are denatured so that they can be grouped into simple categories and more easily dealt with. These are the categories which contemporary economists use to speak of their subject. For example, we can mention the attempt to "commodify" various economic elements which are, properly speaking, not commodities at all. This is the case with *land*, *labor*, and *money*, all of which are examples of what the distributist economist John Médaille has termed the "fictitious commodities."[202]

---

[201] *LS*, 92, 107.

[202] John Médaille, *Toward a Truly Free Market: A Distributist Perspective on the Role of Government, Taxes, Health Care, Deficits, and More* (Wilmington, 2011), p. 70.

Commodities are "reproducible, elastic objects and services that are made mainly to be exchanged in the marketplace."[203] Typically we are able to discern whether or not a thing qualifies as a commodity by observing its behavior on the traditional supply and demand chart. If we can adjust the price and quantity in such a way as to lead to the intersection of the supply and demand curves, we will identify the equilibrium point for this particular market and this will suggest to us that the good or service in question is, or can at least be treated with some accuracy, as a commodity. The three "fictitious commodities" do not respond in a normal way when placed on the supply and demand chart, suggesting that they are not commodities, and that a stubborn insistence on treating them as such will lead inevitably to incoherence in our theory and grave miscalculations in practice.

The failure of this test is a theoretical justification for refusing to consider certain things, such as human labor, as commodities. Yet we would be incorrect to assume that this is the sole reason for rejecting such categorizations. Catholic doctrine refuses to commodify human labor due to the dehumanizing or "objectifying" results of such a mentality, and would continue to reject this attitude on the basis of human dignity even if it were theoretically workable. Such objections will therefore be mentioned in their turn, but it is important for us to acknowledge that the neoclassical view fails in both respects: both morally *and* theoretically. We will now address each of the three fictitious commodities.

a. Land

Land cannot be called a commodity for the simple reason that it is not produced by human labor. Land is that which is *labored upon* in order to produce commodities. It is presupposed by, and is therefore prior to, all economic activities. It can in a limited sense be improved upon or impoverished by human labor, but the notions of production and reproduction break down when applied to it.[204]

---

[203] Ibid., p. 72.
[204] Recall here our previous observations regarding ownership of one's body

If it is to be classified in conventional terms, we could most accurately call it a form of global "capital"; and in fact it is the most primordial form of capital. And although it is possible to price, buy, and sell a piece of land, its unique nature prevents it from behaving as a commodity when subjected to market forces. This is why it has been treated with special consideration throughout history. For example, it is said in the Old Testament: "The land must not be sold permanently, because the land is mine and you reside in my land as foreigners and strangers."[205] Moreover, in the Middle Ages it was the king and the king only, who could be said to "own" any land, and everyone else—dukes, knights, peasants, villains—were only tenants in fealty to the king, who himself was only playing the role (acknowledged as such) of God, who was the true owner.

The tradition of the Jubilee is evidence of the unique nature of land ownership. Moreover, we should also mention another traditional form of land ownership known as the "commons." This form of community ownership, complemented by an emphasis on the equitable distribution of land amongst individual owners, is constantly re-affirmed in CST.[206] In fact the conscientious re-distribution of land is openly encouraged, especially in countries where the concentration of land results in slavery (latifundium).[207]

b. Labor

Much could be, and has been, said about the nature of human work and the dignity which is its due. Nonetheless, in the modern period from the beginning of the industrial age the Christian truth about work has been opposed by various trends of materialistic and economistic thought. The most significant of these has been the desire to turn labor

---

that we do not "own" ourselves as is commonly supposed. One cannot own as chattel what one cannot create.

[205] *Lev* 25:23.

[206] *CSDC,* 180.

[207] *PP,* 23; *CSDC,* 300.

into a commodity, on the assumption that its price ought to be determinable based solely on market factors:

> "For certain supporters of such ideas, work was understood and treated as a sort of 'merchandise' that the worker—especially the industrial worker—sells to the employer, who at the same time is the possessor of the capital, that is to say, of all the working tools and means that make production possible...the danger of treating work as a special kind of 'merchandise', or as an impersonal 'force' needed for production (the expression 'workforce' is in fact in common use) always exists, especially when the whole way of looking at the question of economics is marked by the premises of materialistic economism."[208]

The quote above was taken from *Laborem Exercens*, promulgated by St. John Paull II in 1981. Ten years later, in *Centesimus Annus*, he applauded those who had successfully integrated these principles into their political outlook, attempting to "deliver work from the mere condition of 'a commodity' ":

> "...we see in some countries and under certain aspects a positive effort to rebuild a democratic society inspired by social justice, so as to deprive Communism of the revolutionary potential represented by masses of people subjected to exploitation and oppression. In general, such attempts endeavour to preserve free market mechanisms, ensuring, by means of a stable currency and the harmony of social relations, the conditions for steady and healthy economic growth in which people through their own work can build a better future for themselves and their families. At the same time, these attempts try to avoid making market mechanisms the only point of reference for social life, and they tend to subject them to public control which upholds the principle of the common destination of material goods. In this context, an abundance of work opportunities, a solid system of social security and professional

---

[208] *LE*, 7.

training, the freedom to join trade unions and the effective action of unions, the assistance provided in cases of unemployment, the opportunities for democratic participation in the life of society—all these are meant to deliver work from the mere condition of 'a commodity', and to guarantee its dignity."[209]

The subject of labor will remain a constant theme throughout the remainder of our study.

c. Money

"Money must serve, not rule!"[210] But money cannot be kept in its place, and indeed money will always rule, if its nature and purpose is misunderstood or if it becomes a tool for the exclusive use and manipulation of a specific class.

In our experience a great deal of the disagreement regarding monetary policy stems from misconceptions, confusions, and a general lack of knowledge concerning the nature of money itself. When faced with the question, "What is money?" it seems that most of us have dealt with it, as a concept, for so long that we take its nature as something commonsense; but if we stop to consider it in any detail, we realize that we have no idea how our money system actually functions. Thus, at the risk of digressing too far from our subject, we will attempt a brief description of money and its behavior under the present system.

i. **The nature and purpose of money.** Money is not wealth, but rather it represents wealth. It is a unit of account used in trade which represents a claim on the circulating wealth in the economy. All money is therefore *fiat* currency, which means that it is created "out of nothing" and established by social agreement.

What establishes a currency as "official" is the fact that it is declared legal tender and accepted by the government for the payment of

---

[209] *CA*, 19.
[210] *EG*, 58.

taxes. This ensures that money will always retain at least some value. This also hints at the method of regulation of the money supply: when the government needs the money supply to shrink, it can tax the money out of existence—when the money supply needs to grow, the government can simply "spend" new money into the economy. This creates a "dynamic" and adjustable money supply.

A dynamic money supply is an essential component of a stable economy for the simple reason that economies are subject to constant fluctuations. A simplistic example may suffice:

Imagine that in some village the only product on the market is wheat, and that the harvest one year is 1,000 bushels. The community adopts a paper currency and prints $1,000 dollars. In this situation, $1.00 amounts to a claim on 1 bushel of wheat. This is the value of that dollar. But the next year a farmer develops a new method of crop rotation or fertilization and the village produces 2,000 bushels of wheat. This means that the economy doubled in size. In this situation, if the money supply remains at $1,000, the value of the currency will double, leading to unfortunate results in terms of savings and outstanding loans. That's why, if the village economists are paying attention, they will simply spend another $1,000 into the economy, perhaps on infrastructure or education. The money supply will then grow in proportion with economy. By ensuring that the money supply mirrors the market, the market will remain stable. If, on the other hand, the village economists had adopted gold or some other commodity-money, they would suffer chaos since the quantity of gold is not adjustable but is tied directly to supply. Under a "gold standard" the value of the currency would not be able to adjust itself in accordance with the market, and values would be thrown askew. In short, the economy would become subject to the vicissitudes of inflation and deflation.

This is why, even if it sounds counter-intuitive, the quantity of money must be capable of shrinking or expanding, because the economy itself is always shrinking or expanding—more so as markets become larger and more complex. This is why attempts to adopt static (or mostly static) commodities as official currency—gold, for instance—are doomed to failure. These commodities can be monopolized or scarce. The supply then falls out of sync with the market as a whole, at which point the value of the money rises or falls without any necessary connection to the needs of the market. Money's only purpose is to facilitate trade, and under these conditions it will instead disrupt it. The market itself will become subject to the supply of gold, or whatever commodity happens to be in use as currency.

ii. Money as a commodity. As we said above, money is not meant to be traded: it is meant to *facilitate trade*. This means it is not something manufactured for a market, even though it has no meaning apart from the market. That there is such a thing as a "money market" is itself a sign of dysfunction. When money comes to be treated as a commodity—when we come to believe we can "put our money to work" for us—we are left with a situation where those with an accumulation of money also have a virtual accumulation of goods which they are encouraged to "sell" at a price in order to make a profit. Individual's begin to "rent out" their money, just as you'd rent out a car and charging for its use. In other words, those who have money can loan it out and collect *interest*.

This is not the same as investment—for in investment it is assumed that one's earnings will be proportional to the profits of the endeavor. If the endeavor turns out to be unprofitable then the investor gets no income. But when interest is collected on money without regard to the profits earned from its actual use, this is called *usury*, and has been condemned by everyone from Moses to Christ to the medieval Church, even if it has become the basis of the entire modern economy. The most significant problem with a system in which usury is normalized is that it automatically stacks the deck against the poor. If money makes money, then the more money you have, the more you will be in a position to make. Those with more will make more while those with less will make less, and this will create a perpetual disadvantage in the market toward those who are least in a position to bear that disadvantage. Likewise it will confer perpetual benefit on those which have least need of the advantage.

iv. The fractional reserve system. It is possible to go one step further, not only tolerating usury but adopting it as a basis for the money system itself. This is precisely what has occurred in the contemporary economy in the form of the *fractional reserve system.* Henry Ford found this system so absurd that he famously remarked that, were the American people to understand it, there would be a revolution before breakfast.

The method of this system is implied in the name: "fractional reserve banking." Within this system a bank is only required to have on deposit a small fraction of what they loan, say 10%. For example, if you were to deposit $10,000 in the bank, the bank would be required to keep $1,000 "on reserve." The bank could then create loans for the remaining $9,000. However, *none of the original deposit is actually loaned out.* This is why, when you go back to the bank, they will never reply: "Sorry, your money is on loan." On the contrary, they simply "create" the new loan amount as a debit in the borrowers account. The $9,000 of created loan money now counts as a new deposit on the banks books, and so the bank now has $19,000 "on deposit," even though the original deposit was only $10,000. In addition, this means that $900 of the imaginary money will be marked for the 10% reserve, and then the rest of the "deposit" can be used to create another loan for $8,100. Again, this "new money" is not subtracted from the deposits, but is instead created by a flick of the pen as a new debit in the bank's books. Again and again, 10% of the new deposit will be marked for reserve and the rest used to create loans, and so on, until the original deposit of $10,000 is transformed by fractional reserve magic into $90,000. Almost all of this consists of purely imaginary loans on the bank's books. And on all of this debt, created out of thin air, the bank collects interest.

This process, although we have simplified it somewhat for our purposes here, is how money is created in the modern economy. This means that the videos you watched in school that showed actual paper dollars rolling off of the presses in "the mint" actually do not at all represent the real process of money creation. Paper money only makes up about 3% of the money supply. The other 97% is created through fractional reserve banking, for the benefit of the banks, and on which these banks collect interest.

v. Money as debt. The observant reader will have already realized that under such a system *almost all circulating money is actually debt.* The dollars you have in your bank account actually represent the balance of a loan that you or someone else took out at some point and which was itself based on nothing but a charter granted to a private bank.

Now this is, of course, quite in accordance with the concept of money as a thing *created out of nothing* ("fiat"), except that it has been perverted and rendered dysfunctional. In healthy cases the fiat currency is adjusted (increased or diminished) based on the requirements of the economy, while in the case of the fractional reserve system, the nation is placed in such a position as to be required to *borrow the use of its own money*...at interest to private banks. In such a system the banks own the money supply and the rest of the nation rents it.

Needless to say, this short-circuits the public purpose of an adjustable money supply and instead creates what is called a "perverse incentive" on the part of the banks to create as many loans as possible, because every new loan means new income in the form of interest. Not only does this destroy the stability of the money supply, but it also makes the risk of the credit market completely one-sided. Even if it looks at the outset like banks do take on risk since borrowers could always default, but the results of the 2008 collapse have proven that what actually happens in such systems is quite different. When borrowers default, the banks, being "too big to fail," are simply bailed out by the State, which is to say, by the taxpayers. For the borrower it is a lose-lose, and for the banker it is a win-win. And at the root of the whole system is a validation of the same usurious principles that have been condemned through the millennia.

vi. Possibilities. Keeping in view the fact that the Church does not deal in technical solutions, we must restrict ourselves to the presentation of the system as it is, and the brief mention of alternatives which seem to conform to the principles of reason and the Christian tradition. It is not our purpose here to argue in favor of any one solution, or to suggest such a technical preference on the part of the Church. While it seems quite clear that the fractional reserve system is incompatible with the doctrines of the Church, any suggestions above pertaining to what might be an appropriate solution should be taken as simplistic and offered merely for the purposes of contrast. That is to say, any real solution will be more complicated than the simple abolition of the fractional reserve system, although such an act would be a decent start.

3. Concerning capitalism and socialism

a. The essence of capitalism

The very term "capitalism" signals the nature of its ideological error: just as the "humanist" revolution placed too much exclusive emphasis on the human order, so the capitalist revolution represents one more step down this same path. While humanism shifted emphasis from *God to man*, capitalism shifts emphasis from *man to things*. Traditional civilization had God for its pivot; Renaissance civilization had man; modern civilization has the economy. This last transition amounts to a reversal of the proper hierarchical relationship between material goods and the human being—or capital and labor.

Very early in the development of CST the Church acknowledged the need for cooperation between these two elements in the economic process: "Neither capital can do without labor, nor labor without capital."[211] But man must always maintain priority, and it is precisely this priority that becomes lost through "the development of a one-sidedly materialistic civilization."[212]

Once materialism gains sway, it is only a matter of time before the material component of the economic process supersedes the human one:

> "In all cases of this sort, in every social situation of this type, there is a confusion or even a reversal of the order laid down from the beginning by the words of the Book of Genesis: *man is treated as an instrument of production*, whereas he—he alone, independently of the work he does—ought to be treated as the effective subject of work and its true maker and creator. Precisely this reversal of order, whatever the programme or name under which it occurs, should rightly be called 'capitalism.' "[213]

This particular error will reappear whenever man is,

> "...treated on the same level as the whole complex of the material means of production, as an instrument and not in accordance with the true dignity of his work—that is to say, where he is not treated as subject and maker, and for this very reason as the true purpose of the whole process of production."[214]

Here the reader is encouraged to recall what was emphasized earlier in our discussion of morality, which was that the human subject is never to be treated as a mere *means*.[215] With the nature of man degraded in this way, his relationship with material wealth becomes inverted. Capital then overthrows man as the most significant factor in economic considerations.

---

[211] *RN*, 28.
[212] *LE*, 7.
[213] Ibid.
[214] Ibid.
[215] Section IV, 6d.

b. The separation of ownership from work

Chronologically, as well as logically, this inversion of the relationship between capital and labor is preceded by another more subtle development. In order for capital and labor to be placed in opposition, they first must become *distinct*. For example, the man who owns his own shop and works from within it as its proprietor could never conceive of his activity as a duality of "capital and labor." For him such an antimony does not exist. In order for the capital-labor duality to come into existence, he must assume one of the roles and abdicate the other. For example, he may transition into the role of an owner who pays employees to run his business instead of running it himself. In such a case, he limits his role to that of proprietor of the establishment (capital) and hires wage-workers (labor) for the day to day maintenance of the place, filling orders, keeping shop, etc. Now and only now do we begin to see the two parties mentioned above—one representing capital and the other labor.

Further, because capitalism takes competition as a positive force in its theory, it exacerbates this division. Thus, we find Leo XIII lamenting the fact that "the hiring of labor and the conduct of trade are concentrated in the hands of comparatively few; so that a small number of very rich men have been able to lay upon the teeming masses of the laboring poor a yoke little better than that of slavery itself."[216] Here are sown the seeds of concentration, inequality and strife.

c. Forces of concentration unleashed

Isaiah issued a warning to the Israelites: "Woe to you that join house to house and lay field to field, even to the end of the place: shall you alone dwell in the midst of the earth?"[217]

Clearly, then, the Christian aversion to the concentration of ownership and wealth has ancient roots. It should therefore not come as a surprise when the popes waste no time in condemning it. In order for the

---

[216] *RN*, 3.
[217] *Isa* 5:8.

principle of private property to be realized, economic systems that favor concentration are to be avoided. This is because a society in which only a few possess property is one in which the institution of property is diseased, for how could it be considered healthy when, for the majority of men it does not exist? What is called for are "centrifugal" forces in the economy as opposed to the "centripetal" forces of capitalism.[218]

d. Capitalism as economic liberalism

The popes use the terms capitalism and liberalism almost interchangeably and always with a negative connotation:

> "[W]e are witnessing a renewal of the liberal ideology. This current asserts itself both in the name of economic efficiency, and for the defense of the individual against the increasingly overwhelming hold of organizations, and as a reaction against the totalitarian tendencies of political powers. Certainly, personal initiative must be maintained and developed. But do not Christians who take this path tend to idealize liberalism in their turn, making it a proclamation in favor of freedom? They would like a new model, more adapted to present-day conditions, while easily forgetting that at the very root of philosophical liberalism is an erroneous affirmation of the autonomy of the individual in his activity, his motivation and the exercise of his liberty."[219]

This "erroneous affirmation of the autonomy of the individual" lies at the heart of capitalism's praise for individualism, self-interest, and competition which leads to social Darwinism.

e. Socialism as the child of capitalism

Clearly there is no place in CST for the capitalist ideology. But at the same time we must be careful to avoid that even greater error, which arose as a false cure for the capitalist disease, a cure that was worse than the disease itself, called socialism:

---

[218] *OA*, 44.
[219] *OA*, 35.

"To remedy these wrongs the socialists, working on the poor man's envy of the rich, are striving to do away with private property, and contend that individual possessions should become the common property of all, to be administered by the State or by municipal bodies. They hold that by thus transferring property from private individuals to the community, the present mischievous state of things will be set to rights, inasmuch as each citizen will then get his fair share of whatever there is to enjoy. But their contentions are so clearly powerless to end the controversy that were they carried into effect the working man himself would be among the first to suffer. They are, moreover, emphatically unjust, for they would rob the lawful possessor, distort the functions of the State, and create utter confusion in the community"[220]

These words come from Leo XIII who would later be praised by Pius XI for his rejection of both liberalism (capitalism) and socialism: "He sought no help from either Liberalism or Socialism, for the one had proved that it was utterly unable to solve the social problem aright, and the other, proposing a remedy far worse than the evil itself, would have plunged human society into great dangers."[221] "...let all remember that Liberalism is the father of this Socialism that is pervading morality and culture and that Bolshevism will be its heir."[222] Liberalism as used within this context, and as we always find it within CST, refers directly to the ideological tenets of capitalism, which is simply another name for economic liberalism.

f. Capitalism and socialism as two ideologies to be avoided

The following passage from *Economic Justice for All* embodies the attitude of CST toward the extremes of ideology:

"Some people argue that an unfettered free-market economy, where owners, workers, and consumers pursue their enlightened self-

---

[220] *RN*, 4.
[221] *QA*, 10.
[222] *QA*, 122.

interest, provides the greatest possible liberty, material welfare, and equity. The policy implication of this view is to intervene in the economy as little as possible because it is such a delicate mechanism that any attempt to improve it is likely to have the opposite effect. Others argue that the capitalist system is inherently inequitable and therefore contradictory to the demands of Christian morality, for it is based on acquisitiveness, competition, and self-centered individualism. They assert that capitalism is fatally flawed and must be replaced by a radically different system that abolishes private property, the profit motive, and the free market. Catholic social teaching has traditionally rejected these ideological extremes because they are likely to produce results contrary to human dignity and economic justice."[223]

CST is the guardian of the "invariable middle"—the "narrow way"—which is to say CST promotes the universal principles of truth and justice and is in this sense immune to the tunnel vision of ideology, which always emphasizes one truth to the expense of all others.

g. Against forms of materialistic 'economism'

In order to summarize the complaint the Church places at the feet of both capitalism and socialism, we can refer to the broad notion of *economism*. Economism is the reduction of all social concerns to the economic or material level, on the assumption that if the economy succeeds, all other social goods will be fulfilled as a result. While rarely acknowledged openly and adopted as such, this sort of economism is very common in practice. This is true even for those nations who would still explicitly deny materialism in its doctrinaire form.

Once economism becomes the ruling attitude of a society, its "image" of man is automatically defaced. St. John Paul II describes the historical development of this process as follows:

---

[223] *Economic Justice for All*, 128-129.

"This *consistent image,* in which the principle of the primacy of person over things is strictly preserved, *was broken up in human thought,* sometimes after a long period of incubation in practical living. The break occurred in such a way that labour was separated from capital and set in opposition to it, and capital was set in opposition to labour, as though they were two impersonal forces, two production factors juxtaposed in the same 'economistic' perspective. This way of stating the issue contained a fundamental error, what we can call *the error of economism,* that of considering human labour solely according to its economic purpose. This fundamental error of thought can and must be called *an error of materialism,* in that economism directly or indirectly includes a conviction of the primacy and superiority of the material, and directly or indirectly places the spiritual and the personal (man's activity, moral values and such matters) in a position of subordination to material reality. This is still not *theoretical materialism* in the full sense of the term, but it is certainly *practical materialism,* a materialism judged capable of satisfying man's needs, not so much on the grounds of premises derived from materialist theory, as on the grounds of a particular way of evaluating things, and so on the grounds of a certain hierarchy of goods based on the greater immediate attractiveness of what is material."[224]

h. The doctrine of diffused property

The Church's proposed solution to these errors is based on the nature and needs of man, and can now be put forth in three short quotes from *Rerum Novarum.* It embodies the idea of a "centrifugal" economy in which widely distributed property is the norm.

First Leo XIII notes the sad conditions brought on by unrestrained capitalism:

"...the hiring of labor and the conduct of trade are concentrated in the hands of comparatively few; so that a small number of very rich

---

[224] *LE,* 13.

men have been able to lay upon the teeming masses of the laboring poor a yoke little better than that of slavery itself."[225]

Then he condemns the Marxist solution:

"To remedy these wrongs the socialists, working on the poor man's envy of the rich, are striving to do away with private property, and contend that individual possessions should become the common property of all... But their contentions are so clearly powerless to end the controversy that were they carried into effect the working man himself would be among the first to suffer."[226]

Finally, he proposes the true solution, which is opposed to both capitalism and socialism:

"...private ownership must be held sacred and inviolable. The law, therefore, should favor ownership, and its policy should be to induce as many as possible of the people to become owners."[227]

4. Human Work

a. Good work

"Work is a good thing for man—a good thing for his humanity— because through work man *not only transforms nature,* adapting it to his own needs, but he also *achieves fulfilment* as a human being and indeed, in a sense, becomes 'more a human being.' "[228]

Work, much like the Sabbath, was made for man, and not man for work.[229] It is a good. And not only is work good, but it is also an obligation:

---

[225] *RN,* 3.
[226] *RN,* 4.
[227] *RN,* 46.
[228] *LE,* 9.
[229] *LS,* 128.

"Work is, as has been said, *an obligation,* that is to say, a *duty, on the part of man. . .* Man must work, both because the Creator has commanded it and because of his own humanity, which requires work in order to be maintained and developed. Man must work out of regard for others, especially his own family, but also for the society he belongs to, the country of which he is a child, and the whole human family of which he is a member, since he is the heir to the work of generations and at the same time a sharer in building the future of those who will come after him in the succession of history."[230]

Because he senses these goods, we can assume that under normal circumstances man *desires* to work. He is not inherently lazy, as the social pessimists would have us believe. He feels compelled to action through the drive to develop his faculties and exercise his personality through productive activity. This is what work is for, and it is through the fulfilment of this purpose, and not merely by providing for material needs, that work is considered good. Devoid of these "supra-economic" benefits, work is not good because it is no longer *human.* Considered as a means of material production *and nothing else,* work becomes mere mindless toil.

The fact that in modern times men are taught to be grateful for any kind of work whatsoever, simply because it is more or less "productive," is evidence of an idolatry of work.[231] That it is possible for there to be work which is productive yet not good does not find a place in our thinking, but it is found in Christian philosophy. C.S. Lewis acknowledged it, and not many would call C.S. Lewis a pessimist:

"...the great mass of men in all fully industrialized societies are the victims of a situation which almost excludes the idea of Good Work from the outside...Unless an article is so made that it will go to pieces in a year or two and thus have to be replaced, you will not get a sufficient turnover. A hundred years ago, when a man got

---

[230] *LE,* 16.
[231] *SRS,* 28.

married, he had built for him (if he were rich enough) a carriage in which he expected to drive for the rest of his life. He now buys a car which he expects to sell again in two years. Work nowadays must *not* be good."[232]

Lewis provides two examples—prostitution and advertising—which he classes together as analogous (although not morally equivalent).[233] The point is that for work to be good, it needs to fulfill certain subjective needs of the human being in addition to producing a good effect in the material world.[234]

b. Subjective and objective purposes of work

Distinctions are important, and since the battle against modern ideology is mainly a battle for lost distinctions, a significant part of our project is the re-introduction of subtlety into the economic framework. This is of particular importance when we are discussing the value of human work, which, unlike purely mechanical "work" as executed by machinery, must be considered from both its subjective and its objective points of view, each of which have a legitimate purpose.

The objective meaning of work is the most familiar to us, and in fact it is often the only meaning which has been retained in the present day. Its meaning is embodied in the command to "subdue the earth" and finds expression in the cultivation of crops, the domestication of animals, and the perfection of technology for the purposes of forming the material powers of creation according to man's will.[235] The great successes of science and research, fully embraced by the Church within their proper limits, each play a part in the realization of the objective meaning of work.

---

[232] C.S. Lewis, "Good Work and Good Works," *The World's Last Night and other essays.*
[233] Ibid.
[234] *SRS,* 29.
[235] *LE,* 5.

If we turn now to the concept of work in its subjective sense, we find ourselves in territory that seems a bit more alien to us. And yet, returning to the command to "subdue the earth," which pertains to the objective meaning of work, we realize that it is only in the subjective sense that we can understand *why* man is given this command. *By what right* does he subdue creation? Here we find that the objective meaning presupposes a responsible subject, which is to say *a person*:

> "Man has to subdue the earth and dominate it, because as the 'image of God' he is a person, that is to say, a subjective being capable of acting in a planned and rational way, capable of deciding about himself, and with a tendency to self-realization. *As a person, man is therefore the subject of work.* As a person he works, he performs various actions belonging to the work process; independently of their objective content, these actions must all serve to realize his humanity, to fulfil the calling to be a person that is his by reason of his very humanity."[236]

The truth that the "sources of the dignity of work are to be sought primarily in the subjective dimension, not in the objective one,"[237] are at the heart of the Christian tradition. We must ask first if the work is human, and only then can we begin to measure its industrial efficiency. Our ignorance of the priority of the subjective element, which is to say the primacy of the person in work, is further evidence of the inversion of principles which takes place once the economistic mentality grips a civilization.

c. Direct and indirect employers

Another useful second distinction, the absence of which has proven particularly harmful in application, is between *direct* and *indirect* employers:

---

[236] *LE*, 6.
[237] Ibid.

"The distinction between the direct and the indirect employer is seen to be very important when one considers both the way in which labour is actually organized and the possibility of the formation of just or unjust relationships in the field of labour."[238]

It has become the custom to acknowledge only the *direct* employer, so much so that today when anyone deals with the concept of employment, this is the only type of employment they mean. If we re-introduce the concept of the indirect employer, we are immediately forced to acknowledge the very real interdependence between nations, as well as between individuals within a nation. What, then, is the meaning of these two terms?

"Since the direct employer is the person or institution with whom the worker enters directly into a work contract in accordance with definite conditions, we must understand as the indirect employer many different factors, other than the direct employer, that exercise a determining influence on the shaping both of the work contract and, consequently, of just or unjust relationships in the field of human labour...The concept of indirect employer includes both persons and institutions of various kinds, and also collective labour contracts and the *principles* of conduct which are laid down by these persons and institutions and which determine the whole socioeconomic *system* or are its result."[239]

While the indirect employer is composed of a certain aggregate of social and political elements, it is nonetheless a distinct entity which must be acknowledged for the role it plays in economic action. And because both the direct and indirect employers have legitimate roles, they also have their respective duties which must be fulfilled simultaneously:

"The responsibility of the indirect employer differs from that of the direct employer—the term itself indicates that the responsibility is

---

[238] *LE*, 16.
[239] *LE*, 16-17.

less direct—but it remains a true responsibility: the indirect employer substantially determines one or other facet of the labour relationship, thus conditioning the conduct of the direct employer when the latter determines in concrete terms the actual work contract and labour relations. This is not to absolve the direct employer from his own responsibility, but only to draw attention to the whole network of influences that condition his conduct. When it is a question of establishing an ethically correct labour policy, all these influences must be kept in mind. A policy is correct when the objective rights of the worker are fully respected."

"The concept of indirect employer is applicable to every society, and in the first place to the State. For it is the State that must conduct a just labour policy."[240]

In short, because political society forms the overarching framework in which labor agreements, working conditions, and wages are determined, it has a responsibility above and beyond that of the "direct employer" when it comes to the formation and direction of those agreements. This is a necessary consideration before proceeding to the specific agreement between employer and employee—the agreement called the "labor contract."[241]

d. Agreements between employer and employee

In our discussion of justice we distinguished between commutative, distributive, and social justice. The direct agreements between employer and employee fall under the domain of commutative justice, which is the justice of exchange and is the most basic order of economic justice. However, these agreements must meet certain conditions beyond "mutual consent" in order to be considered just. They are not automatically just simply because the employer offered the contract and the employee accepted, for the right of the worker is not something

---

[240] *LE*, 17.
[241] See also: *LE*, 18-19.

determined by the worker himself, but is determined by an objective standard:

> "Let the working man and the employer make free agreements, and in particular let them agree freely as to the wages; nevertheless, there underlies a dictate of natural justice more imperious and ancient than any bargain between man and man, namely, that wages ought not to be insufficient to support a frugal and well-behaved wage-earner. If through necessity or fear of a worse evil the workman accept harder conditions because an employer or contractor will afford him no better, he is made the victim of force and injustice."[242]

In addition to commutative justice, this contract must be capable of taking into consideration the requirements of distributive and social justice.[243] This is the "political logic" which must participate in and guide all "economic logic":

> "Economic life undoubtedly requires contracts, in order to regulate relations of exchange between goods of equivalent value. But it also needs just laws and forms of redistribution governed by politics, and what is more, it needs works redolent of the spirit of gift. The economy in the global era seems to privilege the former logic, that of contractual exchange, but directly or indirectly it also demonstrates its need for the other two: political logic, and the logic of the unconditional gift."[244]

e. Stakeholders over shareholders

We would also be remiss if we neglected to mention the role of investment in the contemporary economic situation, which is acknowledge by the Church in its teachings. In order to consider it

---

[242] *RN*, 45.

[243] *CV*, 35.

[244] *CV*, 37.

properly, however, we must introduce a third distinction, pointing out the difference between *shareholders* and *stakeholders*.[245]

> "Without doubt, one of the greatest risks for businesses is that they are almost exclusively answerable to their investors, thereby limiting their social value. Owing to their growth in scale and the need for more and more capital, it is becoming increasingly rare for business enterprises to be in the hands of a stable director who feels responsible in the long term, not just the short term, for the life and the results of his company, and it is becoming increasingly rare for businesses to depend on a single territory. Moreover, the so-called outsourcing of production can weaken the company's sense of responsibility towards the stakeholders—namely the workers, the suppliers, the consumers, the natural environment and broader society—in favour of the shareholders, who are not tied to a specific geographical area and who therefore enjoy extraordinary mobility. Today's international capital market offers great freedom of action. Yet there is also increasing awareness of the need for greater social responsibility on the part of business. Even if the ethical considerations that currently inform debate on the social responsibility of the corporate world are not all acceptable from the perspective of the Church's social doctrine, there is nevertheless a growing conviction that business management cannot concern itself only with the interests of the proprietors, but must also assume responsibility for all the other stakeholders who contribute to the life of the business: the workers, the clients, the suppliers of various elements of production, the community of reference."[246]

The variety of points made here cannot be explored individually in detail, but should serve to illustrate the need to make the intended distinction in our economic considerations. That corporate entities can be pressured by "absentee" proprietors with little or no long-term interest in the enterprise and no ties to the geographical area of the

---

[245] On the priority of stakeholders, see *LS*, 183.
[246] *CV*, 40.

business makes for a problematic arrangement for those persons most directly involved in a business's future.

5. Competition or cooperation?

The Church calls for cooperation over and against competition. Dozens of citations could be listed,[247] but we must limit ourselves here to a few. The interested reader will have no problem extending the list on his own.

> "Just as the unity of human society cannot be founded on an opposition of classes, so also the right ordering of economic life cannot be left to a free competition of forces. For from this source, as from a poisoned spring, have originated and spread all the errors of individualist economic teaching. Destroying through forgetfulness or ignorance the social and moral character of economic life, it held that economic life must be considered and treated as altogether free from and independent of public authority, because in the market, i.e., in the free struggle of competitors, it would have a principle of self direction which governs it much more perfectly than would the intervention of any created intellect. But free competition, while justified and certainly useful provided it is kept within certain limits, clearly cannot direct economic life—a truth which the outcome of the application in practice of the tenets of this evil individualistic spirit has more than sufficiently demonstrated."[248]

> "Individual initiative alone and the mere free play of competition could never assure successful development. One must avoid the risk of increasing still more the wealth of the rich and the dominion of the strong, whilst leaving the poor in their misery and adding to the servitude of the oppressed...an economy of exchange can no longer be based solely on the law of free competition, a law which, in its

---

[247] *CSDC*, 420.
[248] *QA*, 88.

turn, too often creates an economic dictatorship. Freedom of trade is fair only if it is subject to the demands of social justice."[249]

With respect to cooperation we may add the following:

"*Economic initiative is an expression of human intelligence and of the necessity of responding to human needs in a creative and cooperative fashion.* Creativity and cooperation are signs of the authentic concept of business competition: a '*cumpetere*', that is, a seeking together of the most appropriate solutions for responding in the best way to needs as they emerge."[250]

6. Self-interest and the profit motive

The two terms which go to form this section's heading amount to spiritual poison for the society that attempts to adopt them as its guiding principles. Man has always been eager to discover that philosophy by which he can consider himself moral without first having to make himself good. It is only very recently that he has finally achieved it, and he did this through the doctrine of self-interest.

Its basic premise is that, if each of us behaves selfishly, then the net outcome will be an increase in overall happiness. We find this at the heart of capitalism, which teaches its adherents that self-interested economic behavior is the engine of the economic progress; we also find it at the heart of sexual libertinism, which teaches that if we would just "leave each to his own," then we would all be happier and better off. Both teach men to think of egoism as a sort of indirect path to altruism. By caring only for yourself, and leaving everyone else to do the same, society benefits as a whole, even if you never consciously acted in an unselfish manner. A man can care best for society by caring only for himself. Thus, the Gospel is finally made irrelevant. Even more, if selfishness is believed to be the key to happiness and the engine of progress, then unselfishness becomes a vice and the Gospel is not

---

[249] *PP*, 33 and 59.
[250] *CSDC*, 343.

merely irrelevant but is reversed: its teachings are not just unnecessary, but are in fact a menace and must be expelled. Although this may sound like hyperbole, it is precisely what has been done in popular egoistic philosophies like that of Ayn Rand.

a. An expression of consequentialism

Here we begin to understand why it was necessary to dwell on the principles of Catholic morality earlier in our study.[251] We observed that man's concrete action *and the will behind the action* must both be conformed to the good in order for the act to be moral. If self-interest is in itself unhealthy, it does not matter if it produces vast amounts of wealth for the world. *We may not do evil that good may come of it*, and that is all there is to it. There is no praise for the man who "unintentionally" helps society when his only conscious choices were to help himself. The doctrine of self-interest fails not because it lacks productive value (although arguments could certainly be made that it fails here as well), but because of the habit it instill in the soul. *For what good is it for a man to gain the whole world, yet forfeit his soul?*[252]

b. Self-interest fuels the growth of the State

It is also worth mentioning that Aquinas saw the tendency toward self-interest as one of the reasons government must exist. Logically, then, the more selfish the population becomes, the more it will need to be parented by the State. The greater the emphasis on self-interest, the greater the need for a superior authority to look after the common good: "For where there are many men together and each one is looking after his own interest, the multitude would be broken up and scattered unless there were also an agency to take care of what appertains to the commonweal."[253]

In a fully self-interested society, what "agency" is there to look to the commonweal but the totalitarian State? And this is precisely what the

---

[251] See section IV above.
[252] *Mk* 8:36.
[253] *DR*, 8.

Church does not want. The State has a proper sphere, which is larger than some moderns would prefer to admit, but it is forced out of this sphere today by the very individualism that pretends to condemn state-overreach. Through individualism and the doctrine of self-interest, all intermediate groups and associations are torn apart, leaving only the State to pick up the pieces, growing into a behemoth in the process:

> "...things have come to such a pass through the evil of what we have termed 'individualism' that, following upon the overthrow and near extinction of that rich social life which was once highly developed through associations of various kinds, there remain virtually only individuals and the State."[254]

c. Profit motive as the engine of economic growth

Profit undoubtedly has a role to play, both from the standpoint of personal motivation and as reward for labor, and also as a measure of the success of an enterprise. However, when sought for itself alone it becomes greed plain and simple.

> "The principle of the maximization of profits, frequently isolated from other considerations, reflects a misunderstanding of the very concept of the economy."[255]

Not only does the blind pursuit of maximum profit lead to the abuse of workers who must rely on wages for their living,[256] but it can also obscure the fact that profitability does not, in itself, imply that an enterprise is playing a positive role in society.[257] On the contrary, "it is possible for the financial accounts to be in order, and yet for the people—who make up the firm's most valuable asset—to be humiliated and their dignity offended."[258] The goal of profit, legitimate within

---

[254] *QA*, 78.
[255] *LS*, 195.
[256] *LE*, 11.
[257] *CCC*, 2424.
[258] *CA*, 35.

limits and as a measure of the health of a business, must be kept in harmony with the dignity of the person and the proper concern for environmental health, both of which are superior values.[259]

Perhaps the most disconcerting result of an all-embracing desire for profit is the fact that it inevitably excludes all those businesses and individuals who would choose to operate by a different motivation, and this is unjust. "Space also needs to be created within the market for economic activity carried out by subjects who freely choose to act according to principles other than those of pure profit, without sacrificing the production of economic value in the process."[260]

7. Market autonomy and the "free" market

Nowhere in Catholic doctrine do we find support for the absolute autonomy of the market (the idea that the market is capable of "regulating itself" without any interference from outside or above). On the contrary, St. John Paul II claimed that "the conviction that the economy must be autonomous, that it must be shielded from 'influences' of a moral character, has led man to abuse the economic process in a thoroughly destructive way."[261]

While it is legitimate to speak of "autonomy" with respect to economic activities, what is meant is always a relative autonomy, which must be circumscribed within the limits of a superior order, which is to say an ethical order:

> "The Church's social doctrine, while recognizing the market as an irreplaceable instrument for regulating the inner workings of the economic system, points out the need for it to be firmly rooted in its ethical objectives, which ensure and at the same time suitably circumscribe the space within which it can operate autonomously."[262]

---

[259] *LS*, 190.
[260] *CV*, 37.
[261] *CV*, 34.
[262] *CSDC*, 349.

And so we find ultimately that the so-called "free market," a notion which concerns the particular conditions of relative economic freedom in a given political order, are always limited and directed by the needs of the political order. If we allow the relative freedom of the market to become absolutized, then we allow a legitimate good to become transmogrified into a source of evil:

> "All of this can be summed up by repeating once more that economic freedom is only one element of human freedom. When it becomes autonomous, when man is seen more as a producer or consumer of goods than as a subject who produces and consumes in order to live, then economic freedom loses its necessary relationship to the human person and ends up by alienating and oppressing him."[263]

We noted above that any freedom, in order to remain legitimate, must maintain a constant connection with truth and goodness. Likewise, economic freedom must be placed within the overarching context of morality.

8. Morality and economic theory

The Church insists that there are always moral connotations to economic activity.[264] In the words of Benedict XVI, quoted already in an earlier section but worth repeating here: "Every economic decision has a moral consequence."[265] To say this another way, economics cannot, like the physical sciences, be conceived as governed by a system of impersonal laws on which moral judgment has nothing to declare. This is why, until quite recently, the field was called "Political Economy," and never simply "Economics." Moreover, the moral aspect of the market includes not only the typical activities of buying and selling, but

---

[263] *CA*, 39.
[264] *CSDC*, 330-335.
[265] *CV*, 37.

extends also to investments and the use of financial instruments which are becoming ever more abstract and complex.[266] Because justice is central to economic activity, we must not forget to consider justice *in every phase* of that process.[267]

To summarize, we refer to *Quadragesimo Anno*:

> "Even though economics and moral science employs each its own principles in its own sphere, it is, nevertheless, an error to say that the economic and moral orders are so distinct from and alien to each other that the former depends in no way on the latter. Certainly the laws of economics, as they are termed, being based on the very nature of material things and on the capacities of the human body and mind, determine the limits of what productive human effort cannot, and of what it can attain in the economic field and by what means. Yet it is reason itself that clearly shows, on the basis of the individual and social nature of things and of men, the purpose which God ordained for all economic life. But it is only the moral law which, just as it commands us to seek our supreme and last end in the whole scheme of our activity, so likewise commands us to seek directly in each kind of activity those purposes which we know that nature, or rather God the Author of nature, established for that kind of action, and in orderly relationship to subordinate such immediate purposes to our supreme and last end."[268]

9. Consumerism

Through the confusion of quantity with quality, the production and consumption of economic goods comes to be seen as an end in itself. This leads to *consumerism*, a mentality in which it is assumed that "economic growth," by whatever means and without respect to the quality or kind of goods being produced, and without concern for the kind of appeals being made to the public, is always beneficial. Although

---

[266] *CV*, 40; CA, 36.
[267] See section III, 7a-d.
[268] *QA*, 42-43.

this is rooted in a healthy desire to improve man's worldly situation, it quickly transforms into something else:

> "A given culture reveals its overall understanding of life through the choices it makes in production and consumption. It is here that *the phenomenon of consumerism* arises. In singling out new needs and new means to meet them, one must be guided by a comprehensive picture of man which respects all the dimensions of his being and which subordinates his material and instinctive dimensions to his interior and spiritual ones. If, on the contrary, a direct appeal is made to his instincts — while ignoring in various ways the reality of the person as intelligent and free — then *consumer attitudes* and *life-styles* can be created which are objectively improper and often damaging to his physical and spiritual health. Of itself, an economic system does not possess criteria for correctly distinguishing new and higher forms of satisfying human needs from artificial new needs which hinder the formation of a mature personality. *Thus a great deal of educational and cultural work* is urgently needed, including the education of consumers in the responsible use of their power of choice, the formation of a strong sense of responsibility among producers and among people in the mass media in particular, as well as the necessary intervention by public authorities...It is not wrong to want to live better; what is wrong is a style of life which is presumed to be better when it is directed towards 'having' rather than 'being', and which wants to have more, not in order to be more but in order to spend life in enjoyment as an end in itself."[269]

Pope Francis has emphasized this point time and time again,[270] with particular focus on what he calls the "throw away culture."[271]

---

[269] *CA*, 36.
[270] *LS*, 34, 50, 184, 203, 209, 210, 215, 219, 232.
[271] *LS*, 16, 22, 43; *EG*, 53.

10. Intermediate Organizations—Unions

The Church encourages the formation of what it calls "intermediate organizations," "intermediate bodies," or "intermediate associations" which can close the gap between ownership and work that has been created through concentration of property.[272] Often, when mention is made of "civil society," it is precisely these intermediate social groupings that are being referred to.[273] In this sense, such intermediates form the link between families and the State in such a way that the "graduated order" sought by the principle of subsidiarity can be realized to its fullest measure.

Closely related to this call for intermediate organizations, although serving a much more specific purpose, are the workers associations known as *unions*. These unions "grew up from the struggle of the workers—workers in general but especially the industrial workers—to protect their just rights *vis-à-vis* the entrepreneurs and the owners of the means of production."[274] Unions were necessitated when work became divorced from ownership and created a class of men whose only power in the market was price they could get for their physical labor. Because such a situation inevitably puts the laborer at a distinct disadvantage, unions today play a necessary role in society[275] and are considered part of the "right of association":

> "All these rights, together with the need for the workers themselves to secure them, give rise to yet another right: *the right of association,* that is to form associations for the purpose of defending the vital interests of those employed in the various professions. These associations are called labor or trade unions."[276]

11. Just Price

---

[272] *CSDC,* 281.
[273] *CSDC,* 356.
[274] *LE,* 20.
[275] *CSDC,* 305-307.
[276] *LE,* 20.

The conventional wisdom would have us believe the market has the last word when it comes to the value of commodities, and that fluctuations in pricing always correspond to real changes in the value of things based on legitimate demand combined with scarcity or surplus in the supply. Added to the principle of maximum profit, competition, and self-interest, this means that a seller should always seek the highest price, and the buyer the lowest, and that this will naturally lead to a point of equilibrium, and this price located at this point will be the most just. But it should be clear by now that things are never so simple, and that such a simplistic view is the result of ideological thinking in an attempt to convert economic activity into an amoral process between two selfish individuals.

Referring back to St. Thomas Aquinas, we find a different view:

> "It is written (Matthew 7:12): 'All things . . . whatsoever you would that men should do to you, do you also to them.' But no man wishes to buy a thing for more than its worth. Therefore no man should sell a thing to another man for more than its worth."[277]

To take advantage of another's need in order to extract a higher price for an item (which in the conventional view would amount to simply obeying the laws of supply and demand) is immoral because raising the price based on another's circumstances is to attempt to "sell what you do not own." You are claiming the advantages of circumstance as if it were your own labor that brought it about, and on this pretense you are profiting unjustly at your neighbor's expense. Often the disadvantage of one's neighbor has nothing to do with the labor of the craftsman, and is an opportunity for charity rather than for profit. To capitalize on such a situation amounts to a species of fraud:

> "It is altogether sinful to have recourse to deceit in order to sell a thing for more than its just price, because this is to deceive one's neighbor so as to injure him....if the one man derive a great

---

[277] *ST* II-II, q. 77, a. 4.

advantage by becoming possessed of the other man's property, and the seller be not at a loss through being without that thing, the latter ought not to raise the price, because the advantage accruing to the buyer, is not due to the seller, but to a circumstance affecting the buyer. Now no man should sell what is not his, though he may charge for the loss he suffers...On the other hand if a man find that he derives great advantage from something he has bought, he may, of his own accord, pay the seller something over and above: and this pertains to his honesty."[278]

The Church teaches that there is a "just price" which is objectively determinable and which does not depend solely on market conditions and the circumstances of the buyer and seller. The just price is a central principle in the Christian economic tradition. The forces of the market are always to be taken into account, of course, but they are never the only factors. We are assured that in some cases the "prices that are freely agreed upon can turn out to be most unfair. It must be avowed openly that, in this case, the fundamental tenet of liberalism (as it is called), as the norm for market dealings, is open to serious question."[279]

Moreover, we must remember that not all prices are subject to market forces in the same way:

"It would appear that, on the level of individual nations and of international relations, the *free market* is the most efficient instrument for utilizing resources and effectively responding to needs. But this is true only for those needs which are 'solvent', insofar as they are endowed with purchasing power, and for those resources which are 'marketable', insofar as they are capable of obtaining a satisfactory price."[280]

---

[278] Ibid.
[279] *PP*, 58.
[280] *CA*, 34.

The three fictitious commodities (land, labor, money) are all examples of non-marketable resources.

12. Living Wage

Just as there is a just price for commodities, it must be stated even more emphatically that there is a just price for one's labor. This is known in CST as the "living wage":

> "Let the working man and the employer make free agreements, and in particular let them agree freely as to the wages; nevertheless, there underlies a dictate of natural justice more imperious and ancient than any bargain between man and man, namely, that wages ought not to be insufficient to support a frugal and well-behaved wage-earner. If through necessity or fear of a worse evil the workman accept harder conditions because an employer or contractor will afford him no better, he is made the victim of force and injustice."[281]

In fact, St. John Paul II suggested that a low regard for human labor, which causes work to be priced too low, degraded men, led to unemployment, and exacerbated poverty[282]—a point on which he was later affirmed by Benedict XVI.[283]

The living wage is not, therefore, a number. It is a standard of judgment and is elastic. It will change depending on time and place, but this does not mean that it is entirely arbitrary. Whether or not a wage is just can be determined by the application of several measures:

1) Are families in general living at a standard of decency appropriate to their society?

2) Are they able to accomplish this without working extremely long hours?

---

[281] *RN*, 45.
[282] *LE*, 8.
[283] *CV*, 63.

3) Are women and/or children forced to work at inappropriate tasks, at inappropriate hours, or under inappropriate conditions in or for the family to subsist?

4) Can families provision themselves without recourse to government assistance?

5) Can families provision themselves without recourse to consumer credit?

While the actual wage amount that qualifies as *living*, and therefore *just*, may vary, it must always satisfy the demands suggested above. This is why we describe it not as a figure but as a dynamic standard. Also, it should go without saying that this standard requires the application of human judgment and cannot be left to the determinations of the market, which are always stacked in favor of capital and will never result in a just wage.

We can also mention that even in purely economic terms, a living wage is beneficial for a society. Wages pressured always and everywhere to a minimum naturally minimize demand, which leads to recession, which leads to failures in supply, which leads to stagnation. The living wage is therefore a practical as well as a moral principle.

Leo XIII complemented this teaching with an added warning—that it is better, concerning these issues, to have recourse to the intermediate associations which we've already discussed:

> "In these and similar questions, however—such as, for example, the hours of labor in different trades, the sanitary precautions to be observed in factories and workshops, etc.—in order to supersede undue interference on the part of the State, especially as circumstances, times, and localities differ so widely, it is advisable that recourse be had to societies or boards such as We shall mention presently, or to some other mode of safeguarding the interests of the wage-earners; the State being appealed to, should circumstances require, for its sanction and protection."[284]

The reasoning here is of course according to the principle of subsidiarity, and it is appropriate because a local association is in a much better position to determine the needs of the parties involved. Having once more referred to these intermediates, which are unfortunately all too rare in our day, we can illustrate their purpose by adopting a historical example of such an organization: the guild. This will also give us a working example of the other principle related to this economic order.

13. The Guild System

a. The nature of the guild

The term "guild" is largely dead, or is at least devoid of historical meaning where it is still employed. The guilds were not "clubs" of individuals with similar interests, as we might find a "quilting guild" today; nor were they analogous to modern labor unions. In fact, the phrase "labor union" signals the difference: for while modern unions are formed exclusively of *workers* who have nothing but their labor to bargain with, the guilds were formed by "working owners" whose strength lay in their ownership as much as in their labor. Thus, in this respect, we can see that modern unions have been rendered necessary precisely due to the division between ownership and work, or capital and labor, a division which does not make any sense in the guild context.

The guilds, thriving primarily throughout the Middle Ages, were cooperative associations. Neither private nor public, they served the role of the "intermediate organizations" mentioned earlier.[285] By serving as this link between individual and State—a link which no longer exists in contemporary society—craftsmen were able to wield political strength while nonetheless retaining their independence from a distant political authority. As such, they were able to provide for their membership in ways that are unthinkable today.

---

[284] *RN,* 45.

[285] Section III, part 5b; section V, part 10.

In his massive survey of history, Will Durant described how incredibly diverse the divisions were among the crafts, and how organized. He found that the leather industry, for example, had separate guilds for "skinners, tanners, cobblers, harness makers and saddlers." Likewise, among carpenters there were "chest makers, cabinetmakers, boatbuilders, wheelwrights, coopers, twiners," and so on.[286]

As to the functions and features of the guilds, Durant reports that:

> "Guild rules limited the number of masters in an area, and of apprentices to a master; forbade the industrial employment of women except the master's wife, or of men after six P.M.: and punished members for unjust charges, dishonest dealing, and shoddy goods. In many cases the guild proudly stamped its products with its 'trademark' or 'hallmark,' certifying their quality... Competition among masters in quantity of production or price of product was discouraged, lest the cleverest or hardest masters become too rich at the expense of the rest; but competition in quality of product was encouraged among both masters and towns. Craft, like merchant, guilds, built hospitals and schools, provided diverse insurance, succored poor members, dowered their daughters, buried the dead, cared for widows, gave labor as well as funds to building cathedrals and churches, and pictured their craft operations and insignia in cathedral glass." A guild would also often "provide for its members insurance against fire, flood, theft, imprisonment, disability, and old age. It built hospitals, almshouses, orphanages and schools."[287]

Now consider for a moment the astounding level of autonomy exhibited here in this massive project of cooperation. Consider how socially competent these organizations much have been. Notice also that while these groups regulated themselves, they did not do so by verdict of

---

[286] Will Durant, *The Age of Faith* (New York, 1950), p. 635.
[287] Ibid., pp. 635-636.

anonymous and far-removed legislators, but of their own accord based on the principles of justice they perceived. Needless to say, such an accomplishment would be completely impossible under the aegis of self-interest, competition, and maximized profit.

The guilds not only regulated the conditions of work, wages, quality control, and the just price within the trade, but provided equivalents to modern insurance, social security, public works and philanthropy.

b. The Catholic call for a return to the guild principle

We are justified in offering this somewhat detailed examination of the guild system for two reasons:

First, the social teachings of the Church refer repeatedly to this institution by name, so we are assured that whatever it was, the Church generally approved of its existence. Second, the guild system lends itself so well to a point by point application of the principles of CST. Thus, we mention it here not because it was perfect or because we expect the guild system to be resurrected precisely in its historical form—rather, we offer it as an *illustration* in order to show that the principles defended by the Church have been successfully applied in the past. Therefore they could be applied again, even if the new applications do not manifest themselves in precisely the same form as the guilds of the Middle Ages. Our goal is not to transplant an extinct institution into alien soil—for again, CST offers principles and not technical solutions—but to offer a very developed solution that is capable of exemplifying our ideal and proving it as a legitimate possibility.

> "In any case...some opportune remedy must be found quickly for the misery and wretchedness pressing so unjustly on the majority of the working class: for the ancient workingmen's guilds were abolished in the last century, and no other protective organization took their place. Public institutions and the laws set aside the ancient religion. Hence, by degrees it has come to pass that working men have been surrendered, isolated and helpless, to the

hardheartedness of employers and the greed of unchecked competition."[288]

Shortly afterward, St. Pius X would echo a similar call, and for precisely the same reasons, emphasizing the value of history and its examples when it comes to our efforts at solving contemporary problems:

"...since in the clash of interests, and especially in the struggle against dishonest forces, the virtue of man, and even his holiness are not always sufficient to guarantee him his daily bread, and since social structures, through their natural interplay, ought to be devised to thwart the efforts of the unscrupulous and enable all men of good will to attain their legitimate share of temporal happiness, We earnestly desire that you should take an active part in the organization of society with this objective in mind...be convinced that the social question and social science did not arise only yesterday; that the Church and the State, at all times and in happy concert, have raised up fruitful organizations to this end; that the Church, which has never betrayed the happiness of the people by consenting to dubious alliances, does not have to free herself from the past; that all that is needed is to take up again, with the help of the true workers for a social restoration, the organisms which the Revolution shattered, and to adapt them, in the same Christian spirit that inspired them, to the new environment arising from the material development of today's society."[289]

And finally, in perfect unison with his predecessors, Pius XI would make the same call at great length and detail in the celebrated *Quadragesimo Anno*:

"The social policy of the State, therefore, must devote itself to the re-establishment of the Industries and Professions. In actual fact, human society now, for the reason that it is founded on classes with

---

[288] *RN*, 3.
[289] Pius X, Apostolic Mandate.

divergent aims and hence opposed to one another and therefore inclined to enmity and strife, continues to be in a violent condition and is unstable and uncertain.

"Labor, as Our Predecessor explained well in his Encyclical, is not a mere commodity. On the contrary, the worker's human dignity in it must be recognized. It therefore cannot be bought and sold like a commodity. Nevertheless, as the situation now stands, hiring and offering for hire in the so-called labor market separate men into two divisions, as into battle lines, and the contest between these divisions turns the labor market itself almost into a battlefield where, face to face, the opposing lines struggle bitterly. Everyone understands that this grave evil which is plunging all human society to destruction must be remedied as soon as possible. But complete cure will not come until this opposition has been abolished and well-ordered members of the social body - Industries and Professions - are constituted in which men may have their place, not according to the position each has in the labor market but according to the respective social functions which each performs. For under nature's guidance it comes to pass that just as those who are joined together by nearness of habitation establish towns, so those who follow the same industry or profession—whether in the economic or other field—form guilds or associations, so that many are wont to consider these self-governing organizations, if not essential, at least natural to civil society.

"Because order, as St. Thomas well explains, is unity arising from the harmonious arrangement of many objects, a true, genuine social order demands that the various members of a society be united together by some strong bond. This unifying force is present not only in the producing of goods or the rendering of services - in which the employers and employees of an identical Industry or Profession collaborate jointly - but also in that common good, to achieve which all Industries and Professions together ought, each to the best of its ability, to cooperate amicably. And this unity will be the stronger and more effective, the more faithfully individuals and the Industries and Professions themselves strive to do their work and excel in it.

"It is easily deduced from what has been said that the interests common to the whole Industry or Profession should hold first place in these guilds. The most important among these interests is to promote the cooperation in the highest degree of each industry and profession for the sake of the common good of the country. Concerning matters, however, in which particular points, involving advantage or detriment to employers or workers, may require special care and protection, the two parties, when these cases arise, can deliberate separately or as the situation requires reach a decision separately.

"The teaching of Leo XIII on the form of political government, namely, that men are free to choose whatever form they please, provided that proper regard is had for the requirements of justice and of the common good, is equally applicable in due proportion, it is hardly necessary to say, to the guilds of the various industries and professions.

"Moreover, just as inhabitants of a town are wont to found associations with the widest diversity of purposes, which each is quite free to join or not, so those engaged in the same industry or profession will combine with one another into associations equally free for purposes connected in some manner with the pursuit of the calling itself. Since these free associations are clearly and lucidly explained by Our Predecessor of illustrious memory, We consider it enough to emphasize this one point: People are quite free not only to found such associations, which are a matter of private order and private right, but also in respect to them 'freely to adopt the organization and the rules which they judge most appropriate to achieve their purpose.' The same freedom must be asserted for founding associations that go beyond the boundaries of individual callings. And may these free organizations, now flourishing and rejoicing in their salutary fruits, set before themselves the task of preparing the way, in conformity with the mind of Christian social teaching, for those larger and more important guilds, Industries and Professions, which We mentioned before, and make every possible effort to bring them to realization."[290]

c. On adaptation

We wish to remind the reader once more, because the point is easily forgotten, that the Church does not attempt to transplant technical solutions from one period to another, but to defend principles which are timeless. Thus, the popes return again and again to the institution of the guild because of its exceptional value as an illustration. As Leo XIII implored so long ago in *Humanum Genus*:

"[T]here is a matter wisely instituted by our forefathers, but in course of time laid aside, which may now be used as a pattern and form of something similar. We mean the associations of guilds of workmen, for the protection, under the guidance of religion, both of their temporal interests and of their morality. If our ancestors, by long use and experience, felt the benefit of these guilds, our age perhaps will feel it the more by reason of the opportunity which they will give of crushing the power of the sects. Those who support themselves by the labour of their hands, besides being, by their very condition, most worthy above all others of charity and consolation, are also especially exposed to the allurements of men whose ways lie in fraud and deceit. Therefore, they ought to be helped with the greatest possible kindness, and to be invited to join associations that are good, lest they be drawn away to others that are evil. For this reason, We greatly wish, for the salvation of the people, that, under the auspices and patronage of the bishops, and at convenient times, these guilds may be generally restored. To Our great delight, sodalities of this kind and also associations of masters have in many places already been established, having, each class of them, for their object to help the honest workman, to protect and guard his

---

[290] *QA*, 82-87.

children and family, and to promote in them piety, Christian knowledge, and a moral life."[291]

The observant reader will have noticed that, by entering a discussion of the guild and its organizational structure, which is largely extra-economic, we have moved beyond the realm of economic activity and into the political. At this point, then, we can take up that sphere more explicitly.

---

[291] *HG*, 35.

Section VI. Political Society

1. The problem of ideology

Ideology is the first problem to address in any contemporary political discussion. Ideology may be defined as the attempt to answer vast, complex problems by means of simplistic, "common sense," closed systems of thought. Ideologies are always narrow in their approach, promising utopia if only their doctrines can be given full assent and obedience. They provide a false haven from the perennial problems of life, and are in this sense an attempt to escape from the responsibility of real action, choosing instead a vague, abstract, and usually ambiguous solution.[292] The present pope has identified, perhaps more than any of his predecessors, the specific evil of ideology, and has responded by declaring war on this way of thinking.

Pope Francis speaks of ideology as a "distilled faith," passed through a filter with only the superficialities retained. "In ideologies there is not Jesus: in his tenderness, his love, his meekness. And ideologies are rigid, always. Of every sign: rigid. And when a Christian becomes a disciple of the ideology, he has lost the faith: he is no longer a disciple of Jesus, he is a disciple of this attitude of thought."[293]

Socialism and capitalism are two ideologies with which CST struggles most, although it sometimes refers to the first as Marxism, and the second as economic "liberalism." Because the latter—capitalism—is the reigning ideology of the present era, we will develop the Church's teaching on this ideology in particular. It does not matter at all that there is no such thing as pure capitalism *in actuality,* any more than there is pure socialism. That neither of these extremes can be realized in practice does not prevent them from being entertained in the mind as

---

[292] *OA*, 27.

[293]

http://en.radiovaticana.va/storico/2013/10/17/pope_francis_prayer_keeps_us_fr om_losing_faith/en1-738101

erroneous ideals, poisoning the thinking of millions. It is in this latter "idealistic" form that ideologies such as capitalism wreak havoc in modern society. It is also *as ideologies* that Pope Francis condemns them.

a. Liberalism

Paul VI wrote of his period:

> "...we are witnessing a renewal of the liberal ideology. This current asserts itself both in the name of economic efficiency, and for the defense of the individual against the increasingly overwhelming hold of organizations, and as a reaction against the totalitarian tendencies of political powers. Certainly, personal initiative must be maintained and developed. But do not Christians who take this path tend to idealize liberalism in their turn, making it a proclamation in favor of freedom? They would like a new model, more adapted to present-day conditions, while easily forgetting that at the very root of philosophical liberalism is an erroneous affirmation of the autonomy of the individual in his activity, his motivation and the exercise of his liberty."[294]

And so it seems that any contemporary discussion of ideology must give special focus to liberalism, because it represents the operating ideology of the present era. Yet we must be clear about what is meant by the word. As we have already stated above, when the Church refers to "liberalism" she is speaking of that ideology,

> "which believes it exalts individual freedom by withdrawing it from every limitation, by stimulating it through exclusive seeking of interest and power, and by considering social solidarities as more or less automatic consequences of individual initiatives, not as an aim and a major criterion of the value of the social organization."[295]

---

[294] *OA*, 35.
[295] *OA*, 26.

In CST, the Church is usually speaking directly of economic liberalism, which, as we remarked above, is also called capitalism. However, capitalism is only one expression of liberalism, and there are two others with which the Church has done battle in the past: religious liberalism and political liberalism. Recalling the definition of liberalism stated above, it should be obvious that just as capitalism represents the precise application of liberalism in the economic sphere, so the Reformation expressed the same principles in the religious sphere, while birth of secular government represents liberalism in the political sphere. We can identify these three liberal movements as personified by their respective thinkers: Adam Smith in the economic domain, Martin Luther in the religious, and John Locke in the political.

In fact, we could go so far as to say that CST in general represents a prolonged response to the errors of liberalism in the economic sphere.

b. Liberalism is not an American political party

Despite the way the term is used in the United States, when the popes speak of liberalism they are not fighting against the American Democratic Party. They have something much larger in mind. No doubt, of course, the American "liberals" are products of the liberal ideology, as evidenced by their preference for secularism in political affairs and their insistence on the absolutism of certain political rights; however, American "conservatives" are just as much children of liberalism as their counterparts, what with their intemperate devotion to the autonomy of markets, combined with their insistence on the absolutism of property rights. The two American parties are both thoroughly liberal—they simply represent two different sides of the coin.

2. The true purpose of the State

Government is a divinely instituted good. Solomon says that "Where there is no governor, the people shall fall."[296] And Paul warns that there

---

[296] *Eccl* 4:9.

is no authority except that which God has established.[297] Yet it is also true that the State exists for man, and not man for the State.[298] God established authority, but for man and not for itself.

If we apply the principles of solidarity and subsidiarity, we can sum up the purpose of the State by saying that it is to serve the common good by fulfilling those requirements which cannot be met by lower associations. These can be roughly enumerated as keeping the peace between lower social bodies, providing for defense from foreign invaders, and seeing to the maintenance of distributive justice. In a healthy society the role of the State need not be extensive or overly intrusive. The State is, however, completely necessary. Only in society can man fulfill himself, and this means that political life is part of his nature. Social and political activities are justified in their existence because of man, and should not be viewed as something erected over and against him.

It does not follow from this that the government which governs least, governs best.[299] The opposite may just as often prove true. The State has a distinct role to play, and it must be judged, not based on how much or little it governs, but by whether or not it carries out the functions proper to it. It "exists to achieve an end otherwise unobtainable: the full growth of each of its members, called to cooperate steadfastly for the attainment of the common good, under the impulse of their natural inclinations towards what is true and good."[300]

3. The end of the State must coincide with the end of man

Because the State exists to assist man in realizing the potentialities of his nature, and because his vocation is in its noblest sense a spiritual one,

---

[297] *Rom* 13:1.
[298] *CCC*, 1881; *GS*, 25.
[299] *Economic Justice for All*, 124.
[300] *CSDC*, 384.

then political society fails automatically if it does not take into consideration anything more than the temporal lives of its citizens.[301] As it has been put by Aquinas:

> "[T]he same judgment is to be formed about the end of society as a whole as about the end of one man...If such an ultimate end either of an individual man or a multitude were a corporeal one, namely, life and health of body, to govern would then be a physician's charge. If that ultimate end were an abundance of wealth, then knowledge of economics would have the last word in the community's government. If the good of the knowledge of truth were of such a kind that the multitude might attain to it, the king would have to be a teacher. It is, however, clear that the end of a multitude gathered together is to live virtuously. For men form a group for the purpose of *living well* together, a thing which the individual man living alone could not attain, and *good life* is virtuous life. Therefore, virtuous life is the end for which men gather together...Yet through virtuous living man is further ordained to a higher end, which consists in the enjoyment of God...Consequently, since society must have the same end as the individual man, it is not the ultimate end of an assembled multitude to live virtuously, but through virtuous living to attain to the possession of God."[302]

Now these words should not be interpreted as a demand for State-run churches, mandatory attendance of the mass, and the like. Aquinas is merely acknowledging the fact that the State, since it plays the governing role in society, cannot make pretenses at spiritual indifference. Let it try to adopt the stance of indifferentism, and it will end by establishing a practical atheism.

So what might Aquinas's vision look like in practice? To take but one example, the Church calls on the State to ensure that workers have a

---

[301] *CSDC*, 386.
[302] *DR*, 106-107.

sufficient amount of rest, not merely to repair the strain placed on the body during labor, but so that workers can properly devote themselves to their spiritual exercises which can easily fall into neglect. Man must therefore be provided with rest for both soul and body, and not for the body alone.[303] By such simple measures we can see how the State ought to act in favor of the religious life without assuming responsibility for it.

4. The relations between Church and State

In attempting to reconcile the ends of man with the ends of the State, we are brought to an examination of the proper relationship between the Church and the State. Because of the timeliness of this subject, and because it appears frequently in contemporary political debates, we will dwell on it at length.

a. Liberal secularism and practical atheism

The problem with liberal secularism, which is the governing mentality in most modern States, including the U.S., is that such regimes attempt to take a stance of indifference toward religion. Unfortunately, as we mentioned above, a purely negative stance toward religion is not in reality a neutral one, as is supposed; to stand aloof and refuse to make affirmative statements about religion inevitably leads to a positive exclusion of religion from all public considerations, even if this was not necessarily the intention the founders of such regimes. On this point, Leo XIII is in agreement:

> "To hold, therefore, that there is no difference in matters of religion between forms that are unlike each other, and even contrary to each other, most clearly leads in the end to the rejection of all religion in both theory and practice. And this is the same thing as atheism, however it may differ from it in name."[304]

In short, liberal regimes are based on the absurd idea that a man can have freedom *of* religion while his neighbor has an equal share of

---

[303] *RN*, 41-42.
[304] *ID*, 31.

freedom *from* religion, as if the two ought never to come into conflict. For this to be true, the two men would essentially have to live entirely in isolation from one another, which is to say they would have to cease to live in the same community.

The expression of one's religion will always come into direct conflict with the *freedom from religion*. It is of its very nature to find social expression. There is no such thing as "private religion." Thus, to create a society that exists *free for*, and at the same time *free from*, religion is impossible. For the State to choose not to choose is for it to adopt a negative position against all positive positions, and this negative position is atheism. Even agnosticism, for the State, is not a possibility.

b. Leo XIII on the separation of Church and State

It is for this reason that the Church has always insisted that the State absolutely cannot make pretenses at neutrality. The State must not only acknowledge God, but must acknowledge the Christian God. There can be no separation between church and state in the modern sense, as the following excerpts from Leo XIII's *Libertas* clearly show:

> "There are others, somewhat more moderate though not more consistent, who affirm that the morality of individuals is to be guided by the divine law, but not the morality of the State, for that in public affairs the commands of God may be passed over, and may be entirely disregarded in the framing of laws. Hence follows the fatal theory of the need of separation between Church and State. But the absurdity of such a position is manifest. Nature herself proclaims the necessity of the State providing means and opportunities whereby the community may be enabled to live properly, that is to say, according to the laws of God. For, since God is the source of all goodness and justice, it is absolutely ridiculous that the State should pay no attention to these laws or render them abortive by contrary enact menu. Besides, those who are in authority owe it to the commonwealth not only to provide for its external well-being and the conveniences of life, but still more to consult the welfare of men's souls in the wisdom of their legislation. But, for the increase of such benefits, nothing more suitable can be

conceived than the laws which have God for their author; and, therefore, they who in their government of the State take no account of these laws abuse political power by causing it to deviate from its proper end and from what nature itself prescribes. And, what is still more important, and what We have more than once pointed out, although the civil authority has not the same proximate end as the spiritual, nor proceeds on the same lines, nevertheless in the exercise of their separate powers they must occasionally meet. For their subjects are the same, and not infrequently they deal with the same objects, though in different ways. Whenever this occurs, since a state of conflict is absurd and manifestly repugnant to the most wise ordinance of God, there must necessarily exist some order or mode of procedure to remove the occasions of difference and contention, and to secure harmony in all things. This harmony has been not inaptly compared to that which exists between the body and the soul for the well-being of both one and the other, the separation of which brings irremediable harm to the body, since it extinguishes its very life."[305]

"For, to reject the supreme authority to God, and to cast off all obedience to Him in public matters, or even in private and domestic affairs, is the greatest perversion of liberty and the worst kind of liberalism...From this teaching, as from its source and principle, flows that fatal principle of the separation of Church and State; whereas it is, on the contrary, clear that the two powers, though dissimilar in functions and unequal in degree, ought nevertheless to live in concord, by harmony in their action and the faithful discharge of their respective duties."[306]

"Many wish the State to be separated from the Church wholly and entirely, so that with regard to every right of human society, in institutions, customs, and laws, the offices of State, and the education of youth, they would pay no more regard to the Church

---

[305] *LP*, 18.
[306] *LP*, 37-38.

than if she did not exist; and, at most, would allow the citizens individually to attend to their religion in private if so minded. *Against such as these, all the arguments by which We disprove the principle of separation of Church and State are conclusive; with this super-added, that it is absurd the citizen should respect the Church, while the State may hold her in contempt.*"[307]

c. Martin Luther on the separation of Church and State

The notion of a beneficial "wall of separation between church and state" has its roots in liberal philosophy, and in fact this idea follows very naturally from its basic premises. So inevitable was this conclusion that we find it rearing its head not only in the political philosophies of John Locke and J.S. Mill, but even from religious reformers such as Martin Luther, who advised princes as follows:

"...you have people under you and you wish to know what to do. It is not Christ you are to question concerning the matter but the law of your country...Between the Christian and the ruler, a profound separation must be made...Assuredly, a prince can be a Christian, but it is not as a Christian that he ought to govern. As a ruler, he is not called a Christian, but a prince. The man is a Christian, but his function does not concern his religion...Though they are found in the man, the two states or functions are perfectly marked off, one from the other, and really opposed."[308]

And while the Catholic Church had warned kings that "through this crown, you become a sharer in our ministry,"[309] the secularism of Luther was to become the unconscious *status quo* in all the later liberal-democratic regimes with which Protestantism would form an unhealthy union. In nations built on this philosophy, even those Catholics who wished to participate in public life would have to sacrifice their principles to the liberal altar. Consider the following statements of the

---

[307] *LP*, 39. Emphasis added.
[308] *Luther's Works* (Wiemar Edition) XXXII, pp. 391, 439, 440.
[309] Bertrand de Jouvenel, *On Power* (Indianapolis, 1976), p. 33.

Catholic president, John F. Kennedy, and consider how perfectly they mirror the thinking of Luther, while at the same time flatly contradicting the teachings of Kennedy's own Church:

> "I believe in an America where the separation of church and state is absolute... I am not the Catholic candidate for president. I am the Democratic Party's candidate for president, who happens also to be a Catholic. I do not speak for my church on public matters, and the church does not speak for me...Whatever issue may come before me as president—on birth control, divorce, censorship, gambling or any other subject—I will make my decision...in accordance with what my conscience tells me to be the national interest, and without regard to outside religious pressures or dictates."[310]

d. Confession versus coercion

Now it seems wise to remind the reader of that document which we mentioned early on in our discussion, namely *Dignitatis Humanae*. There is a very distinct difference between confession of faith on the part of the State, and acts of coercion by it. The confession of faith by a public authority need not entail—and in fact must not entail—coercion of the citizen with respect to religion, for the conscience of the individual is a thing that cannot be coerced. *Dignitatis Humanae* therefore affirms the Church's traditional condemnation of the latter, while at the same time it "leaves untouched traditional Catholic doctrine on the moral duty of men and societies toward the true religion and toward the one Church of Christ."[311]

As an example of this arrangement working in a healthy manner, which is also proof that *Dignitatis Humanae* was not revolutionary in its nature, we might remind the reader of the role of the Church in combating popular oppressions in the past, such as those against the Jews and against women accused of witchcraft. Churchmen of the

---

[310] *Address to the Greater Houston Ministerial Association* delivered Sept. 12, 1960.
[311] *DH*, 1.

Inquisition itself were some of the most determined voices in attempts to curb the persecution of "witches" and "sorcerers" in Europe. Pope Alexander IV even declared a canon prohibiting even the investigation of alleged witches.

As a counterexample to show what happens when popular movements are allowed to go unchecked by an active spiritual authority, the Salem witch trials in the United States can teach us a great deal.

Returning again to the issue of conscience, we must remember that Leo XIII, that towering warrior against the political errors of liberalism who is himself cited in *Dignitatis Humanae*, vigorously stated his agreement with Vatican II's position, saying that "the Church is wont to take earnest heed that no one shall be forced to embrace the Catholic faith against his will, for, as St. Augustine wisely reminds us, 'Man cannot believe otherwise than of his own will.' "[312]

5. Peace or strife?

Now we come to an issue of competition in political affairs, which is closely related to our discussion of capitalist societies. Earlier it was addressed in its economic form. Here we address it as a much broader mentality, because our economic attitudes never remain in the purely economic sphere, but expand and invade every area of life.

After the fashion of capitalism and the theory of evolution, modern society believes that strife is an intrinsic good. It is *the* mechanism for progress. In science, for example, it is believed that human life itself is the result of a perpetual struggle for existence, a "survival of the fittest" through which progress is brought about. This same attitude appears in economic ideologies which hold competition to be the engine of social welfare and human creativity. Likewise, in political institutions there is a sort of "institutionalized conflict" represented by the separate branches of government and the parties competing for control of those branches. Such a system is *designed for conflict.*

---

[312] *ID*, 36.

In every case, then, it seems that the underlying assumption is that peace follows from chaos, and that strife is the mother of harmony. Because this has become so engrained as to seem natural, it may surprise the reader to find that the Church—and indeed most other traditions outside of modern systems—taught the opposite: that peace is the supreme value to be sought and strife avoided;[313] and that this is in fact a duty which must be acted upon and not left as if it would occur as a result of automatic processes.[314]

a. True peace is harmony of wills

The peace in question is not the peace which follows combat, which is simply the peace of death and defeat. The peace sought by the Christian is not merely the absence of war, pain, or the precarious tension of "balanced powers." True peace is a harmonious union of wills through which those involved not only cease to fight, but actually agree in their desires. Such persons are "unified" in their efforts. Peaceful unity requires the courageousness of trust, the seeking of justice, the practice of love, and the realization of human brotherhood.[315] In fact, we can say that peace is more the fruit of love than of justice, since justice removes obstacles to peace, while it is the part of love to bring it to fruition.[316]

It goes without saying that if strife is considered the ideal and peace simply a *consequence* of the mechanism of strife, then true peace will be perpetually undermined. War and threat of war cannot be escaped so long as sin persists, but this does not in any way transform them into goods to be sought after as if they were the engines of peace, for this would only bring about the peace of death.

---

[313] John Paull II, *Message for the 1982 World Day of Peace*, 4.
[314] Ibid.
[315] *GS*, 78.
[316] *UA*, 35; *ST* II-II, q. 29, a. 3, ad. 3.

b. On obedience and revolution

We are sometimes led to believe that the philosophers and theologians of old demanded an unconditional submission to social authorities. We also imagine that this was motivated by the naïve assumption that social authorities were divinely instituted and therefore unconditionally legitimate. In truth, however, men like Aquinas always acknowledged the existence of legitimate causes for the removal of unjust rulers. The difference between the traditional thinking and the modern has more to do with the circumstances that each accepts as "unjust."

For example, while moderns tend to view revolution as legitimate virtually any time the governed become dissatisfied with their government. So long as it can be clearly demonstrated that the people are unhappy—a majority vote, for example—a leader can be removed. All that is required is proof that it was the will of the people. The justification for removal of leaders in democratic regimes, then, boils down to a question, not of some objective standard of justice, but of public opinion plain and simple.

It is on this point that the thinkers of the Middle Ages beg to differ. For them, because governmental authority was instituted, not personally but universally and by God, its operation had to be judged by a standard of justice that was objective, like God. If a ruler was to be removed, he had to be removed by proving that he was governing unjustly. If he was carrying out his functions well, it would not matter if 99% of the population wanted him removed, it would be unjust to do so.

To simplify the problem, we can make the distinction between the ruler himself, as an individual, and the office that he is holding. Respect is due to a ruler because he is holding an office. Thus, the respect he is given is less due to him *personally* as it is due to the divinely ordained authority, which is to say, to God as represented by him. *Even if he behaves ignobly, he holds a noble office.* So when is it appropriate to remove an ignoble noble? Taking into account this separation between the man (who may be good or evil) and the office (which, being divinely instituted, is in itself good), we can say with the theorists of the

Middle Ages that it is legitimate to remove even a good man who is a bad ruler, but it is not legitimate to remove a bad man who is a good ruler.

Such is the meaning of Christ's words to the apostles: "The scribes and the Pharisees sit in Moses' seat: All therefore whatsoever they bid you observe, that observe and do; but do not ye after their works: for they say, and do not."[317] Thus, when it comes to bad men who are good leaders, we are told to do what they say but not what they do. The most obvious implication here is that, although Christ bluntly acknowledged hypocrisy, he also commanded obedience.

6. Issues pertaining to rights and duties

a. State as protector of rights.

Since the rise of Lockean liberalism, it has become common to imagine that the purpose of the State is nothing more than to act as "mediator of rights" between individuals, and that it should not concern itself in the promotion of any particular good beyond this simple role of safeguarding individual liberties. Unfortunately, this has never been the Catholic view of the purpose of political authority—or, more accurately, the Catholic view includes the protection of rights as a purpose of the State,[318] but it refuses to limit the State to this alone, as if it had no other duty.

Moreover, when the Church speaks of the maintenance of the "rights" of citizens, it usually has other things in mind than those mentioned in political conversation today. The right to meaningful work, the right to education, and the right to food and water, are all notions which the Church has in view when it asks to State to guarantee certain fundamental rights.

---

[317] *Mt*, 23:2-3.
[318] *PT*, 273.

The role of the State is an active one—not merely mediating between individuals who exercise their liberties in opposition. It is called to play a positive role in creating an environment where rights *and duties* can be exercised in their fullness.[319]

b. Free of speech and the press

The Church teaches that rights, while valid, not necessarily absolute. Each must be held to the standard of *truth* and limited according to the *common good,* particularly when it comes to its exercise in the public sphere. Apart from truth and the common good, rights tend to undermine themselves and will virtually cease to exist through their own excess. The right of free speech serves as a good example here, as enunciated by Leo XIII:

> "We must now consider briefly liberty of speech, and liberty of the press. It is hardly necessary to say that there can be no such right as this, if it be not used in moderation, and if it pass beyond the bounds and end of all true liberty. For right is a moral power which -- as We have before said and must again and again repeat -- it is absurd to suppose that nature has accorded indifferently to truth and falsehood, to justice and injustice. Men have a right freely and prudently to propagate throughout the State what things soever are true and honorable, so that as many as possible may possess them; but lying opinions, than which no mental plague is greater, and vices which corrupt the heart and moral life should be diligently repressed by public authority, lest they insidiously work the ruin of the State. The excesses of an unbridled intellect, which unfailingly end in the oppression of the untutored multitude, are no less rightly controlled by the authority of the law than are the injuries inflicted by violence upon the weak. And this all the more surely, because by far the greater part of the community is either absolutely unable, or able only with great difficulty, to escape from illusions and deceitful subtleties, especially such as flatter the passions. If unbridled license of speech and of writing be granted to all, nothing will remain

---

[319] *PT,* 274-275.

sacred and inviolate; even the highest and truest mandates of natures, justly held to be the common and noblest heritage of the human race, will not be spared. Thus, truth being gradually obscured by darkness, pernicious and manifold error, as too often happens, will easily prevail. Thus, too, license will gain what liberty loses; for liberty will ever be more free and secure in proportion as license is kept in fuller restraint. In regard, however, to all matter of opinion which God leaves to man's free discussion, full liberty of thought and of speech is naturally within the right of everyone; for such liberty never leads men to suppress the truth, but often to discover it and make it known."[320]

c. Self-ownership

Modern man imagines his body and his "self" as yet one more piece of his private property. The popes, however, suggest otherwise:

> "Not only has God given the earth to man, who must use it with respect for the original good purpose for which it was given, but, man too is God's gift to man. He must therefore respect the natural and moral structure with which he has been endowed."[321]

We have already discussed in-depth the proper understanding of private property,[322] explaining how and why it can never be considered absolute but is itself only one good in a hierarchy of goods, and he who denies the hierarchy destroys its component goods. However, at this point it might be beneficial to refute another modern error which considers the human person, particularly the physical body, as the legal property of the person to whom it belongs. Self-ownership, while true from a particular point of view, is really only a half-truth, and is therefore misleading if adopted blindly as a guiding principle of law. For example, if we adopt this view unquestioningly, we run the risk of having to mediate between the rights of the unborn and the rights of

---

[320] *LP*, 23.

[321] *CA*, 38.

[322] Section III, parts 2 and 3a-c.

mothers, and we are led down a very dark road. Much of this misunderstanding stems from our deeply engrained individualism which tells each man that he is completely responsible for what he is and what he becomes. He therefore ought to consider his own "self" his property. But Benedict XVI puts forth another view:

> "The human person by nature is actively involved in his own development. The development in question is not simply the result of natural mechanisms, since as everybody knows, we are all capable of making free and responsible choices. Nor is it merely at the mercy of our caprice, since we all know that we are a gift, not something self-generated. Our freedom is profoundly shaped by our being, and by its limits. No one shapes his own conscience arbitrarily, but we all build our own "I" on the basis of a "self" which is given to us. Not only are other persons outside our control, but each one of us is outside his or her own control. *A person's development is compromised, if he claims to be solely responsible for producing what he becomes.*"[323]

Pope Francis combats the same mentality, encouraging instead a willing participation in the natural body we have received as a gift from the Creator:

> "...thinking that we enjoy absolute power over our own bodies turns, often subtly, into thinking that we enjoy absolute power over creation. Learning to accept our body, to care for it and to respect its fullest meaning, is an essential element of any genuine human ecology. Also, valuing one's own body in its femininity or masculinity is necessary if I am going to be able to recognize myself in an encounter with someone who is different. In this way we can joyfully accept the specific gifts of another man or woman, the work of God the Creator, and find mutual enrichment."[324]

---

[323] *CV,* 68.
[324] *LS,* 155.

We cannot own ourselves because we are a gift, and the closest a man can come to owning himself is by making a gift of himself to another. Or, in other words, *whosoever wishes to save his life must lose it.*[325] Only by acknowledging this principle of the gift and its primordial role in our very existence can we properly understand the nature of our "ownership" of ourselves. It turns out to be a humbler notion than contemporary political discourse would lead us to believe.

d. The rights of God

Finally, it would not be appropriate to pass over a discussion of rights without acknowledging an unwelcome truth about the tradition of the Church—one that will not sit well with those who have learned to accept without question the separation of church and state, along with the humanistic notions of popular sovereignty and secularism. This unwelcome truth is that society itself, if its notions of freedom are to remain legitimate, must never deny its duty to God, for the rights of God precede the rights of man, and the rights of man cannot persist without this foundation. As Leo XIII stated it: "The world has heard enough of the so-called 'rights of man.' Let it hear something of the rights of God."[326]

And in his encyclical on human liberty, the same pontiff expounded further on the traditional idea of the State and its relationship with religion:

> "God it is who has made man for society, and has placed him in the company of others like himself, so that what was wanting to his nature, and beyond his attainment if left to his own resources, he might obtain by association with others. Wherefore, civil society must acknowledge God as its Founder and Parent, and must obey and reverence His power and authority. Justice therefore forbids, and reason itself forbids, the State to be godless; or to adopt a line of action which would end in godlessness-namely, to treat the various

---

[325] *Mt* 16:25.
[326] *TFP*, 13.

religions (as they call them) alike, and to bestow upon them promiscuously equal rights and privileges. Since, then, the profession of one religion is necessary in the State, that religion must be professed which alone is true, and which can be recognized without difficulty, especially in Catholic States, because the marks of truth are, as it were, engravers upon it. This religion, therefore, the rulers of the State must preserve and protect, if they would provide - as they should do - with prudence and usefulness for the good of the community. For public authority exists for the welfare of those whom it governs; and, although its proximate end is to lead men to the prosperity found in this life, yet, in so doing, it ought not to diminish, but rather to increase, man's capability of attaining to the supreme good in which his everlasting happiness consists: which never can be attained if religion be disregarded."[327]

Here we feel it appropriate to remember the response of the apostles, who, in the face of Christ's words, exclaimed: "This is a hard teaching. Who can accept it?"[328] We may experience this same discomfort at the mention of an acknowledged relationship between the State and the Church. And yet there it remains, comfortable or not.

7. Proper attitudes toward wealth

a. A necessary occasion of sin

Leo XIII warned that "those whom fortune favors are warned that riches do not bring freedom from sorrow and are of no avail for eternal happiness, but rather are obstacles."[329] In saying this, he expressed the traditional attitude of Christianity toward wealth, which is that it represents a "necessary occasion of sin."

Occasions of sin are "external circumstances—whether of things or persons—which either because of their special nature or because of the

---

[327] *LP*, 21.

[328] *Jn* 6:60.

[329] *RN*, 22.

frailty common to humanity or peculiar to some individual, incite or entice one to sin."[330] By calling wealth a "necessary occasion," it is acknowledged that wealth has a valid role to play and that to be wealthy is not, in itself, sinful. Yet wealth does confer a degree of responsibility. It is best to return here to Leo XIII and quote him at length on this aspect of the problem:

> "Therefore, those whom fortune favors are warned that riches do not bring freedom from sorrow and are of no avail for eternal happiness, but rather are obstacles; that the rich should tremble at the threatenings of Jesus Christ—threatenings so unwonted in the mouth of our Lord—and that a most strict account must be given to the Supreme Judge for all we possess."[331]

b. The distinction between ownership and use

Implied in the words of Christ is an important point about wealth: the right to private property does not confer the right to use one's property however one sees fit (or refuse to use it, as the case may be). This is the classical distinction between ownership and use. To continue Leo's words:

> "The chief and most excellent rule for the right use of money is one the heathen philosophers hinted at, but which the Church has traced out clearly, and has not only made known to men's minds, but has impressed upon their lives. It rests on the principle that it is one thing to have a right to the possession of money and another to have a right to use money as one wills. Private ownership, as we have seen, is the natural right of man, and to exercise that right, especially as members of society, is not only lawful, but absolutely necessary. 'It is lawful,' says St. Thomas Aquinas, 'for a man to hold private property; and it is also necessary for the carrying on of human existence.' But if the question be asked: How must one's

---

[330] Delany, Joseph. "Occasions of Sin." *The Catholic Encyclopedia*, Vol. 11. New York: Robert Appleton Company, 1911. 19 Dec. 2014.
[331] *RN*, 22.

possessions be used? - the Church replies without hesitation in the words of the same holy Doctor: 'Man should not consider his material possessions as his own, but as common to all, so as to share them without hesitation when others are in need. Whence the Apostle with, 'Command the rich of this world... to offer with no stint, to apportion largely.' True, no one is commanded to distribute to others that which is required for his own needs and those of his household; nor even to give away what is reasonably required to keep up becomingly his condition in life, 'for no one ought to live other than becomingly.' But, when what necessity demands has been supplied, and one's standing fairly taken thought for, it becomes a duty to give to the indigent out of what remains over. 'Of that which remaineth, give alms.' "[332]

c. Private charity vs. government action

Leo's distinction between ownership and use comes to our aid in many contemporary debates. For example, much is made today of the role of "private charity" when it comes to succoring the poor and needy. Some go so far as to say that, if we would only cut government programs and leave the taxes which support them to be used at the discretion of the taxpayer, then the problem of poverty would be alleviated more efficiently. Let us, then, put forward the Catholic understanding, first of charity itself, and then of the State's role in the task of relieving poverty.

d. Justice before charity

First, although charity is normally considered something of a "private virtue," to be cultivated by the individual rather than coerced by the State, we must also recognize that it still operates in relation to justice, and justice itself has the prior claim. What this means is that if the requirements of justice are not met, then charity has not yet entered the picture, and so what the State extracts from the rich in terms of taxes is not necessarily a matter of coerced charity, but of coerced justice.

---

[332] *RN,* 22.

Coerced charity would be inappropriate, but coerced justice is not. In the words of Benedict XVI, charity goes beyond justice:

> "Charity goes beyond justice, because to love is to give, to offer what is 'mine' to the other; but it never lacks justice, which prompts us to give the other what is 'his', what is due to him by reason of his being or his acting. I cannot 'give' what is mine to the other, without first giving him what pertains to him in justice. If we love others with charity, then first of all we are just towards them. Not only is justice not extraneous to charity, not only is it not an alternative or parallel path to charity: justice is inseparable from charity, and intrinsic to it. Justice is the primary way of charity or, in Paul VI's words, 'the minimum measure' of it."[333]

The Catechism echoes in agreement, citing various authorities on the subject: "Not to enable the poor to share in our goods is to steal from them and deprive them of life. The goods we possess are not ours, but theirs."[334] "The demands of justice must be satisfied first of all; that which is already due in justice is not to be offered as a gift of charity."[335] "When we attend to the needs of those in want, we give them what is theirs, not ours. More than performing works of mercy, we are paying a debt of justice."[336]

Those who try to place charity in opposition to justice, and to use the one to escape the other, are trying to divide two sides of one coin:

> "There is no gap between love of neighbour and desire for justice. To contrast the two is to distort both love and justice. Indeed, the meaning of mercy completes the meaning of justice by preventing justice from shutting itself up within the circle of revenge."[337]

---

[333] *CV*, 6; *PP*, 22; *GS*, 69; Pope Paul IV, *Address for the Day of Development* (23 August 1968).

[334] St. John Chrysostom, Hom. In Lazaro 2, 5: PG 48, 992.

[335] *AA*, 8, 5.

[336] St. Gregory the Great, *Regula Pastoralis*. 3, 21: PL 77, 87.

e. "You didn't build that."

Perhaps it is the attitude of the "meritocracy" which leads to the perceived opposition between charity and justice. It is imagined that nothing is due in justice to anyone who did not "earn" whatever is given to them, and it is suggested that whatever I legally possess is mine purely and simply because I earned it, and it is therefore unjust to suggest that I part from it. But here Scripture gives a warning:

> "When you have eaten and are satisfied, praise the Lord your God for the good land he has given you. Be careful that you do not forget the Lord your God, failing to observe his commands, his laws and his decrees that I am giving you this day. Otherwise, when you eat and are satisfied, when you build fine houses and settle down, and when your herds and flocks grow large and your silver and gold increase and all you have is multiplied, then your heart will become proud and you will forget the Lord your God...You may say to yourself, 'My power and the strength of my hands have produced this wealth for me.' But remember the Lord your God, for it is he who gives you the ability to produce wealth..."[338]

In an absolute sense, all that we have is a gift from God. In a more immediate sense, all that we have is a product of the society in which we live, and in which we've been able to participate, live, learn, labor, and reap fruit. No man is an island, or so the saying goes.

While it is legitimate to lay claim to ownership, and to take credit for the labor one has contributed, it is purely illusory to imagine that we produced everything we have in a vacuum and we owe it to nothing else but our own individual merits. Precisely the same actions, aptitudes, and ideas that can earn a man a fortune in a developed nation, for example, would have very different results in the third world, so preponderant is the role of providence in our accomplishments. St. Ambrose speaks to this:

---

[337] *Libertatis Conscientia*, 57.
[338] *Deut* 8:10-18.

" 'My own', you say? What is your own? When you came from your mother's womb, what wealth did you bring with you? That which is taken by you, beyond what suffices you, is taken by violence. Is it that God is unjust in not distributing the means of life to us equally, so that you should have in abundance while others are in want? Or is it not rather that He wished to confer upon you marks of His kindness, while He crowned your fellow man with the virtue of patience? You, then, who have received the gift of God, think you that you commit no injustice by keeping to yourself alone what would be the means of life to many? It is the bread of the hungry you cling to, it is the clothing of the naked you lock up; the money you bury is the redemption of the poor."[339]

f. The velocity of money

St. Basil likened wealth to a great spring: if the water is drawn frequently, all the purer it will remain; yet if it is left unused it becomes foul and stagnant.[340] Now this is of interest to us because of its economic parallel, which is the concept of the velocity of money. This concept says that money, if it falls into the hands of a poor man, will almost immediately leave his hands, either for rent or for lunch or for some other pressing need. If it goes into the hands of a very wealthy man, it may go into a bank account to draw interest, or it may go nowhere at all for a very long time. Now, economically speaking, the first is best, at least from the standpoint of a healthy, vibrant, functioning economy, while the latter is poisonous and leads to stagnation. The point is that even if the rich man spends and invests with frequency, he cannot possibly equal the velocity of the poor man. And so, at least from a particular point of view, great wealth is very literally a "drag" on the economy, while the more money enters the hands of the needy, the better.

8. Proper attitudes toward poverty

---

[339] Will Durant, *The Age of Faith* (New York, 1950), p. 630.
[340] Cf. Saint Basil the Great, *Homilia in Illud Lucae, Destruam Horrea Mea*, 5

While wealth, properly viewed and handled as a necessary occasion of sin, can be reconciled to the common good, poverty cannot, and therefore it ought to be minimized even if it cannot be eliminated, being one of the ever-present consequences of sin. "The poor you will always have with you," said Christ[341]—but this should never be construed as the "normalization" of poverty, especially since the statement refers to the preciousness of Christ's presence, and not about the tolerability of suffering.[342] What, then, is the appropriate attitude of the Christian toward the issue of poverty?

a. Both the individual and the State have roles to play

First and foremost we need to put behind us the most typical objection to public action on the part of the poor, which says that the public authority ought to leave such things to "private charity," on the assumption that the State has no legitimate interest in the problem—a patently absurd notion, to be sure, but common nonetheless. To this the United States bishops have answered rightly that:

> "The responsibility for alleviating the plight of the poor falls upon all members of society. As individuals, all citizens have a duty to assist the poor through acts of charity and personal commitment. But private charity and voluntary action are not sufficient. We also carry out our moral responsibility to assist and empower the poor by working collectively through government to establish just and effective public policies."[343]

b. Against stigmatizing the poor with stereotypes

Next we must also fight the often vindictive attitude directed toward the poor, as if they were a class to be openly chastised. It would not be difficult to cite numerous passages of scripture that respect, rather than

---

[341] *Mt* 26:11.

[342] For a more lengthy delineation of what follows, as well as for a presentation of principles for action in regard to poverty, see *Economic Justice for All*, 186-214.

[343] *Economic Justice for All*, 189.

resent, the poor for their poverty—that show pity rather than patronization and condescension. In fact we get the impression from any survey of Christian teaching that the traditional sentiment was precisely the opposite of today: in the past it was the poverty which carried signs of holiness along with it, and which seemed to symbolize, even if it did not realize in the individual, the life of Christ. Now, judging by the words and actions of a significant number of individuals, it seems that to be poor is to be automatically guilty of vice, and, as a natural correlative, it is the wealthiest in society who are automatically considered virtuous, and this in proportion to the amount of wealth they accumulate. It is necessary, then, to do away with a few of the common stereotypes that have grown up alongside this reversal of esteem in the Christian attitude toward poverty.[344]

c. Poverty does not imply laziness or disdain for work

It is often insinuated that those on government programs are there as a means of avoiding work, and that these same persons stay on welfare for years even though they could work if they wished. Statistically, none of these assumptions are justified.[345] Many welfare recipients are mothers who must, or have laudably chosen to, remain home to raise their children. Many are elderly. Others are children. Yet mothers are attacked and it is implied that they must have given birth for no other reason than to maintain eligibility for government hand-outs—as if any clear-thinking person would not realize that it would be much easier to work a conventional job than it is to raise children at home. Moreover, research has shown that the poor show the same desire to work as any other social class. We ought to plead with the American bishops against these misguided opinions:

> "We ask everyone to refrain from actions, words or attitudes that stigmatize the poor, that exaggerate the benefits received by the poor, and that inflate the amount of fraud in welfare payments. These are symptoms of a punitive attitude toward the poor."[346]

---

[344] *Economic Justice for All*, 193.
[345] Ibid.

The bishops have duly noted the hypocrisy in this attitude by observing that the most substantial subsidies "handed out" by the government go, not to the lower class, but to individuals and corporations who are by no means in poverty. Yet criticism directed at hand-outs to the already-rich is hardly ever mentioned. Through this selective outrage it becomes obvious that the aforementioned opinions do not stem from any real knowledge of foul play on the part of the poor, but rather from negative attitudes—especially fear—in the hearts of those who do not belong to the lowly class.

d. "Hunger is a great motivator."

We have all heard it suggested, either on the radio or by some person on the street, that it is good for the poor and the unemployed to be under threat of hunger or some other tribulation. This is because, we are told, the threat of suffering is what motivates these slothful creatures to engage in productive labor, and if this threat were removed then the problem of poverty would only become worse. But again, common experience and reflection show clearly that this attitude is false. Very few people limit their productive labor to those hours for which they are remunerated. Most men, when arriving home from "work," simply transition to work on some other project. As was said above, the healthy individual strives to work. Those who would claim that "hunger is a great motivator" would rarely admit that they need this motivation themselves. What's worse, the saying implies that poverty is a *problem of motivation*, and through this implication it allows the speaker to avoid altogether the moral demands which the problem of poverty makes on him and his society. It is an escape from responsibility to the poor by absurdly presenting poverty itself as the best cure for poverty.

e. "He who will not work, neither shall he eat."

It has been said that the devil himself is happy to quote the Scriptures, so long as he can quote it to suit his own purposes. This seems to be the

---

[346] *Economic Justice for All*, 194.

only explanation for the immense popularity of Paul's statement to the Thessalonians: "He who will not work, neither shall he eat."[347]

All that need be said of this matter is that there are countless Scriptures which instruct us on the attitude we are to have toward the poor, and this is not one of them. In fact, when taken in context, it has nothing at all to do with the poor. Paul is speaking to men who quite obviously are in no danger of starvation. Therefore, while his warning certainly speaks against sloth, it would be a malicious error to treat all Scriptures against sloth as if they pertained directly to the poor, as if the poor are the only beings capable of committing this sin.

9. Taxes

It would be naïve to act as if there were a time when men were happy to pay their taxes. However, the collection of taxes, in itself, has never been questioned by the Church as a just procedure—and Christ himself, moreover, did not give us much reason to suspect that Caesar ought not to receive his due.[348] And so, although there are too many factors at play for us to dictate what is and is not a just *tax rate*, we can at least mention a couple of the guidelines insisted upon by the Church in this matter.

a. The justice of a progressive tax system

The first principle, certainly not popular in contemporary ideological schools, concerns the idea that tax revenues ought to be drawn only from those who can afford it, and in greater quantities from those who reap the greatest benefits from the economic system in which they live. In the words of Pius XI's encyclical, *Divini Redemptoris*:

> "It must likewise be the special care of the State to create those material conditions of life without which an orderly society cannot exist...To achieve this end demanded by the pressing needs of the common welfare, the wealthy classes must be induced to assume

---

[347] 2 *Thess* 3:10.
[348] *Mk* 12:17; *Mt* 22:15-22.

those burdens without which human society cannot be saved nor they themselves remain secure. However, measures taken by the State with this end in view ought to be of such a nature that they will really affect those who actually possess more than their share of capital resources, and who continue to accumulate them to the grievous detriment of others."[349]

Needless to say, the exact application of this principle could take various forms, but one can say without much risk of error that the system known as the "progressive tax" is a fairly straightforward and appropriate means of realizing this goal. And this was precisely the interpretation of the USCCB when it said,

"the tax system should be structured according to the principle of progressivity, so that those with relatively greater financial resources pay a higher rate of taxation. The inclusion of such a principle in tax policies is an important means of reducing the severe inequalities of income and wealth in the nation. Action should be taken to reduce or offset the fact that most sales taxes and payroll taxes place a disproportionate burden on those with lower incomes."[350]

b. The poor should not pay income tax

A second guideline, related to the first, is that the government ought to exempt those below the poverty line from any income taxes whatsoever, because such families are, "by definition, without sufficient resources to purchase the basic necessities of life. They should not be forced to bear the additional burden of paying income taxes."[351]

10. Inequality and redistribution

Central to the Biblical concept of the Jubilee is the redistribution of property to alleviate accumulations and dispossession. Such

---

[349] *DR*, 75.
[350] *Economic Justice for All*, 202.
[351] Ibid.

concentration occurs very naturally in many economies, since none are perfect, but it becomes greatly exaggerated in industrialized nations: "The development model of industrialized societies is capable of producing huge quantities of wealth, but also has serious shortcomings when it comes to the equitable redistribution of its fruits and the promotion of growth in less developed areas."[352]

There is an overwhelming amount of time spent in CST exhorting authorities and private persons to act against rising social inequality.[353] Pope Francis has gone so far as calling inequality "the root of all social evil."[354] And if we grant the interdependence of political and economic power, which implies that inequality of property necessarily implies imbalances in political power, then it is not difficult to see why this is so.

a. A problem of distributive justice

We discussed above the differences between commutative and distributive justice. Commutative justice is the most personal, practical, and obvious, but it is also the imprecise. Considering every day transactions, even if both parties aim with good will toward the just price of the goods or services being exchanged, they will rarely hit the mark. When someone under- or over-pays, the amount of the deviation begins to accumulate, introducing disequilibrium into the system. On a social level, when these accumulations reach a certain point, an offense against distributive justice becomes apparent and, because distributive justice is the role of the State, and because it is obvious that at this point only the State could possibly remedy the injustice, it falls to political action to propose a solution. Note that we have only mentioned transactions in which men sincerely aimed at the just price. Even here we must admit that deviations must occur and accumulate. What would

---

[352] Pontifical Council for Justice and Peace, *Towards a better distribution of land*, 1.

[353] *EG,* 52-53, 59-60, 202; *RN,* 3; *PP,* 9; *CV,* 22, 32, 42; *SRS,* 14; *CSDC* 94, 145, 192, 297, 362, 363, 374, 389, 561.

[354] This comment appeared on the Pope's twitter account on April 28, 2014.

we expect, then, in a society in which men are taught to use every means at their disposal to pay least and charge the most in economic transactions?—and in which some are in a position to exploit and some are in a position to be exploited? A society which has forgotten the Just Price in favor of self-interest and the profit-motive will necessitate the action of the State far more than a society which seeks justice of its own accord, because it will be *actively seeking disequilibrium in every transaction.* The need for distributive justice in the case of large-scale inequality is great indeed.

b. Removing structural causes of inequality

Benedict XVI called for the "structural causes of economic dysfunction."[355] He was joined later by Pope Francis who said:

> "As long as the problems of the poor are not radically resolved by rejecting the absolute autonomy of markets and financial speculation and by attacking the structural causes of inequality, no solution will be found for the world's problems or, for that matter, to any problems. Inequality is the root of social ills."[356]

On this point, Francis went so far as to issue a challenge by invoking the words of Christ: "You yourselves give them something to eat!"[357]

But what does this mean?—and what did these popes have in mind? We can begin by remarking that many of the modern world's problems are self-inflicted and are rooted in the imperfection of human planning and problem of selfishness:

> "Having become his own centre, sinful man tends to assert himself and to satisfy his desire for the infinite by the use of things: wealth, power and pleasure, despising other people and robbing them unjustly and treating them as objects or instruments. Thus he makes

---

[355] Benedict XVI, *Address to the Diplomatic Corps,* 8 January 2007.
[356] *EG,* 188.
[357] *Mk* 6:37.

his own contribution to the creation of those very structures of exploitation and slavery which he claims to condemn."[358]

Yet, even if we allow that this diagnosis is accurate, we still need a more specific analysis if we hope to arrive at practical solutions. For this purpose, a cursory survey of CST will produce quite a few more specific causes of inequality: land concentration and the need for agrarian reform, particular for undeveloped nations[359]; unemployment and underemployment; insurmountable barriers to market entry; barriers to education[360]; media preference and prohibitive advertising costs which inevitably favor the few and exclude the majority.[361] With respect to this last point, we can speak of a population of "information rich" which corresponds to an "information poor,"[362] a problem which stems from the unequal availability of technology. Lastly, all of these possibilities involve or encourage large-scale indebtedness, which can be attributed in part to personal choice, but also in part to necessity.[363]

But perhaps the most recurring problem is one we've already mentioned, and which has proven most difficult to remedy. The evil in question is the concentration of property, and the solution proposed is the *redistribution of property*.

c. Redistribution

As unwelcome as the phrase "redistribution of wealth" may be in certain contemporary circles, it is a common theme in CST. In *Caritas in Veritate*, Benedict XVI said that:

---

[358] Congregation for the Doctrine of the Faith, *Instruction on Christian Freedom and Liberation* (22 March 1986), 42.

[359] Pontifical Council for Justice and Peace, *Towards a Better Distribution of Land. The Challenge of Agrarian Reform* (23 November 1997), 13.

[360] *CSDC*, 314.

[361] *CSDC*, 416.

[362] Pontifical Council for Social Communications, *Ethics in Communications* (4 June 2000), 20.

[363] *CSDC*, 450.

"Economic activity cannot solve all social problems through the simple application of *commercial logic*. This needs to be *directed towards the pursuit of the common good*, for which the political community in particular must also take responsibility. Therefore, it must be borne in mind that grave imbalances are produced when economic action, conceived merely as an engine for wealth creation, is detached from political action, conceived as a means for pursuing justice through redistribution."[364]

Throughout this encyclical he uses the term "redistribution" a total of eight times,[365] even mentioning joyfully the "unprecedented possibility of large-scale redistribution of wealth on a world-wide scale."[366]

Although it should be abundantly clear by now that the Church takes this stance *in favor* of private property rather than *against*, the popes are constantly met with accusations of socialism, as if a call to redistribution was equivalent to the abolition of property altogether. But Benedict XVI is defending nothing other than the doctrine of diffused property which we mentioned earlier and which has its roots in *Rerum Novarum* itself. To quote again, for the sake of convenience, the relevant passage, we see that Leo XIII concurs with Benedict XVI:

"The law, therefore, should favor ownership, and its policy should be to induce as many as possible of the people to become owners."[367]

---

[364] *CV*, 36.
[365] *CV*, 32, 36, 37, 39, 42, 49.
[366] *CV*, 42.
[367] *RN*, 46.

Section VII. Environment

1. A long-standing concern

"Never have we so hurt and mistreated our common home as we have in the last two hundred years." So writes Pope Francis in *Laudato Si'*. And he is not alone. In 1971, Paul VI said: "Due to an ill-considered exploitation of nature, humanity runs the risk, of destroying it and becoming in turn a victim of this degradation." Following this same line of thought, Benedict XVI wrote that:

> "The relationship between individuals or communities and the environment ultimately stems from their relationship with God. When man turns his back on the Creator's plan, he provokes a disorder which has inevitable repercussions on the rest of the created order."[368]

As we will see in what follows, man has a distinct responsibility to minister to God's creation in its entirety. This is particularly important at this time, considering the response Pope Francis has received when speaking on this subject. For example, some writers seem to suggest (as is common among persons who've never taken the time to read the encyclicals themselves), that Pope Francis's *Laudato Si'* represents some new venture on the part of the Church—a departure from its customary range of subject matter.

On the contrary, the *Catechism* states that "creation comes forth from God's goodness, it shares in that goodness...for God willed creation as a gift addressed to man, an inheritance destined for and entrusted to him."[369] Through creation we find life, realize our potentialities, come

---

[368] *Letter to the Ecumenical Patriarch of Constantinople on the Occasion of the Seventh Symposium of the Religion, Science and the Environment Movement*, September 1, 2007.
[369] *CCC*, 299.

into relationships with one another, and, through its contemplation, are directed toward God.[370]

In order to drive home the continuity between past popes and Francis, we will pause on his immediate predecessor, who repeatedly emphasized the Church's concern for the environment. To take only a sample of the former pontiff's many statements on this point:

"Preservation of the environment, promotion of sustainable development and particular attention to climate change are matters of grave concern for the entire human family."[371]

"The order of creation demands that a priority be given to those human activities that do not cause irreversible damage to nature, but which instead are woven into the social, cultural, and religious fabric of the different communities. In this way, a sober balance is achieved between consumption and the sustainability of resources."[372]

"The ecological crisis offers a historic opportunity to develop a common plan of action aimed at orienting the model of global development toward greater respect for creation and for an integral human development inspired by the values proper to charity in truth."[373]

"We are all responsible for the protection and care of the environment. This responsibility knows no boundaries. In accordance with the principle of subsidiarity it is important for

---

[370] *CCC,* 287-307.

[371] *Letter to the Ecumenical Patriarch of Constantinople on the Occasion of the Seventh Symposium of the Religion, Science and the Environment Movement,* September 1, 2007.

[372] *Message to the Director General of the Food and Agriculture Organization for the Celebration of World Food Day,* October 16, 2006.

[373] *Message for the Celebration of the World Day of Peace,* January 1, 2010.

everyone to be committed at his or her proper level, working to overcome the prevalence of particular interests."[374]

"The deterioration of nature is... closely connected to the culture that shapes human coexistence: when 'human ecology' is respected within society, environmental ecology also benefits." "The Earth is indeed a precious gift of the Creator who, in designing its intrinsic order, has given us bearings that guide us as stewards of his creation. Precisely from within this framework, the Church considers matters concerning the environment and its protection intimately linked to the theme of integral human development."[375]

If we seem to be over-emphasizing the point, it is only because this issue has been ill-received by certain circles, so much so that it warrants a thoroughly prepared defense on the part of the faithful. The curious reader will have no problem multiplying these references by searching through the many documents provided by the Vatican online.

2. A legitimate concern

Having established a consensus between the popes, we can see that Pope Francis' *Laudato Si'* is simply the latest confirmation on behalf of the Church that the environmental crisis is a very real and legitimate subject of discussion. It can no longer be denied a rightful place in political discourse, and in fact demands our attention. Francis begins his treatment by lamenting that the earth,

"now cries out to us because of the harm we have inflicted on her by our irresponsible use and abuse of the goods with which God has endowed her. We have come to see ourselves as her lords and masters, entitled to plunder her at will. The violence present in our hearts, wounded by sin, is also reflected in the symptoms of sickness evident in the soil, in the water, in the air and in all forms of life."[376]

---

[374] Ibid.
[375] *General Audience*, August 26, 2009.
[376] *LS*, 2.

Nor is it any longer possible to deny the role of human activity in this process. *Nothing in this world is indifferent to us.*[377] Such is the responsibility that is tied with the human dominion over the earth. Other factors may come into play, but it is the human factor which is predominate both as problem and solution.[378]

3. Proper attitudes toward the environment

In a way, by arriving at a discussion of nature and our attitude toward it, we have arrived at the most basic expression of the principle that *grace presupposes nature*. The created universe and the life that unfolds within it are the foundation of existence outside of which grace would have no meaning or way of being brought to fruition. In this sense, we must consider creation as a good, as something given in order to make love between man and God a concrete possibility, and we must respect it as such, and not pretend that it is a dead thing with nothing other than a purely utilitarian value.

Because of this lofty purpose behind creation, our attitude toward it impacts our attitude toward life in general, including our attitude toward ourselves:

> "*The way humanity treats the environment influences the way it treats itself, and vice versa...*Every violation of solidarity and civic friendship harms the environment, just as environmental deterioration in turn upsets relations in society. Nature, especially in our time, is so integrated into the dynamics of society and culture that by now it hardly constitutes an independent variable."[379]

In order to further understand this connection, we can say that the environment is a *collective good*,[380] and is therefore closely linked up with the common good, and so it is fair to say that a disregard for the

---

[377] *LS*, 3.
[378] *LS*, 23.
[379] *CV*, 51; See also *LS*, 92.
[380] *CSDC*, 466.

environment is counter to a basic principle of Catholic Social Teaching. Respect and care for the environment is a duty not only because of the consequences it may have for the living, but because we also are to act as stewards for future generations. In fact, it is no exaggeration to say that we are one with the earth, for our very bodies are made up of its elements. It is through this connection that we can say truly:

> "God has joined us so closely to the world around us that we can feel the desertification of the soil almost as a physical ailment, and the extinction of a species as a painful disfigurement."[381]

We are not given dominion over the earth in order to exploit it at will. Such interpretations of the biblical imperative to "till it and keep it"[382] are perversions of the truth.[383] "If you chance to come upon a bird's nest in any tree or on the ground, with young ones or eggs and the mother sitting upon the young or upon the eggs; you shall not take the mother with the young."[384] The utilization of nature's gifts must be coupled with the restraint of a caring husbandman.

4. A crisis of selfishness

The problem of the environment has its roots in self-centeredness. "The misuse of creation begins when we no longer recognize any higher instance than ourselves, when we see nothing else but ourselves."[385]

This diagnosis points to the only solution, which is the turning away from self toward the world. Francis calls all people of good will "to become painfully aware, to dare to turn what is happening to the world into our own personal suffering and thus to discover what each of us

---

[381] *EG*, 215.
[382] *Gen* 2:15.
[383] *LS*, 66-67.
[384] *Deut* 24:6.
[385] Benedict XVI, *Address to the Clergy of the Diocese of Bolzano-Bressanone (6 August 2008)*.

can do about it."[386] So long as we remain insulated by our egoism, we will remain numb to the consequences of our actions and those of our society on the created order. It is also vital for us to remember that our internalizing the violence done to the environment is not purely an imaginary exercise. The social and the environmental are concretely linked, meaning that what we have before us is not a dichotomy between social and environmental crises, but rather one complex crisis that involves both.[387]

5. Disproportionate responsibilities

"The human environment and the natural environment deteriorate together,"[388] and this deterioration will always take its greatest toll on the weakest members of society. Here, as elsewhere, the principle of the preferential option for the poor must be taken into consideration.[389] This is not only because they are in an economic position that is by definition weak, but also because, on a global level especially, poorer peoples rely more directly on the natural environment for their sustenance when it comes to forestry, agriculture, fishing, etc.

Likewise, because excessive consumption is found, and is in fact sought by, the wealthiest areas of the world, it is only just to recognize that there are "differentiated responsibilities" depending on the needs, lifestyles, and capabilities of a society.[390]

The reality of this disproportion in impact of the environmental crisis explains the tendency of rich nations to deny or ignore the problem entirely. In fact, because the recognition of the problem would result in

---

[386] LS, 19.
[387] LS, 139.
[388] LS, 48.
[389] LS, 25, 48.
[390] LS, 52.

a duty on their part to take action, they have a vested interest in denying its existence.[391] The poor, and not merely the natural environment, become the collateral damage of their indifference.[392] And so Pope Francis reminds us that the questions of society and ecology cannot be separated, but that the earth and her poor cry out in unified suffering.[393]

6. Against economism and short-sightedness

Much of the problem comes from the tendency of the economy, which automatically prioritizes short-term benefits, to overrule any long-term considerations.[394] This is to be expected once the economic interests take precedence over political and social interests. As a result, "whatever is fragile, like the environment, is defenceless before the interests of a deified market, which becomes the only rule."[395] This allows government officials, businessmen, and all other economic participants to blind themselves to the reality of their situation.

> "Such evasiveness serves as a licence to carrying on with our present lifestyles and models of production and consumption. This is the way human beings contrive to feed their self-destructive vices: trying not to see them, trying not to acknowledge them, delaying the important decisions and pretending that nothing will happen."[396]

---

[391] *LS*, 26.
[392] *LS*, 49, 123.
[393] Ibid.
[394] *LS*, 54.
[395] *EG*, 56.
[396] *LS*, 59.

7. Values associated with creation

a. Value of resources as capital

The very real deficiencies in the capitalist ideology become especially evident when considering creation itself. If we were to guess that there was one thing that capitalism could understand, it would be capital, but we find that even here it goes immediately astray. Natural resources, for example, are of two kinds: renewable and non-renewable. Non-renewable resources follow the laws of capital—and this is true even if we treat them, not like capital, but like income. What this means is that, just as any business enterprise requires a certain amount of capital in order to sustain itself, so does the operation of any industry presuppose the capital that is present in the earth. Now, any business would become immediately alarmed if their business plan itself called for a constant consumption of its capital, and did not contain any possible means of replenishing this capital. We would see immediately that such an enterprise was doomed to fail, because it was doomed to consume its own capital. We would see immediately that such a business model was "unsustainable." And likewise, any economic theory that chooses not to acknowledge non-renewable resources as a form of capital, but rather chooses to treat them as income to be disposed of at will, is not sustainable either.

And yet the laws of the market place, particularly in the capitalist framework, cannot account for such a thing as non-renewable resources as capital. They are thus doomed to consume their own means until they go under: it is only a matter of time. This is because capitalism presupposes an infinite universe, or at least has no real way of imposing self-limitations required by a finite universe. Because of this inability to acknowledge reality as we find it—that is to say, limited—capitalism has no way of dealing with non-renewable resources, but treats all resources precisely the same: as fuel for production, to be used as heavily and as quickly as profit and efficiency allow. No limit enters into its calculus until it is imposed by reality. There is no such thing as foresight in such a mentality—there is no such thing as consideration for the future—there is only the law of the marketplace, and this law only works in the present, one transaction at a time. If it comes to a conflict between a non-economic consideration, such as the future well-being of a civilization, and present profit, the latter will always take priority. Thus, K.L. Kenrick once reflected, "We did not realize that Capitalism was prepared to destroy the human race in order to save itself."

b. Value as beauty

John Paul II observed that "Our very contact with nature has a deep restorative power; contemplation of its magnificence imparts peace and serenity."[397] This contemplative potential infuses the earth with an effect that is *therapeutic*, and effect that Christ himself was to appreciate.[398] This effect is rendered null and even reversed when the beauty of nature is disfigured. "The earth, our home, is beginning to look more and more like an immense pile of filth."[399] "We were not meant to be inundated by cement, asphalt, glass and metal..."[400]

One of the fundamental ways through which the power and beauty of creation is manifest is through its *diversity*. It is precisely this diversity which is being constantly diminished through the abuse and exploitation of nature:

"Each year sees the disappearance of thousands of plant and animal species which we will never know, which our children will never see, because they have been lost for ever. The great majority become extinct for reasons related to human activity. Because of us, thousands of species will no longer give glory to God by their very existence, nor convey their message to us. We have no such right."[401]

---

[397] St. John Paul II, *Message for the 1990 World Day of Peace*, 14.
[398] *LS*, 97.
[399] *LS*, 21.
[400] *LS*, 44.
[401] *LS*, 33.

The lifestyle of the developed nations of the world is engineering a heritage of ugliness and want for future generations. It is as if the only beauty we acknowledge is that which we have manufactured and which will be necessarily artificial:

> "[A] sober look at our world shows that the degree of human intervention...is actually making our earth less rich and beautiful, ever more limited and grey...We seem to think that we can substitute an irreplaceable and irretrievable beauty with something which we have created ourselves."[402]

Such an attitude is hubris plain and simple. We must keep our limitations ever before us. For example, we must realize that even in those situations where we acknowledge the violence we have done, it is sometimes not within our efforts to reverse the damage. We can replace a deforested zone through the plantation of trees, but the richness of what came before will not be equaled by the homogenous uniformity that we erected in its place.[403] The fragility of nature's beauty is exemplified when yet another species becomes extinct: it shows us again and again that certain beauties are irreplaceable and are in this sense priceless. Their value cannot be calculated.[404]

When dealing with nature we must keep in mind the principle enunciated by St. John Paul II, which was that the unintended consequences of our actions will always outnumber the intended ones.[405]

c. Value as truth

The created world has a further value in that, if properly appreciated, can and does lead us toward the knowledge of higher things. It is an expression of truth.[406] "For since the creation of the world God's

---

[402] *LS*, 34.

[403] *LS*, 39.

[404] *LS*, 36.

[405] *VS*, 77.

[406] *CV*, 49.

invisible qualities—his eternal power and divine nature—have been clearly seen, being understood from what has been made."[407] "Hence, there is a mystical meaning to be found in a leaf, in a mountain trail, in a dewdrop, in a poor person's face."[408] Indeed, in a very real sense "all things are God."[409]

According to St. Thomas Aquinas, this is not to be taken as some sort of vague sentimentalism, but is a necessary truth about human knowledge. From the material world, we can be directed to invisible truths. Moreover, this invites us to a consideration of every aspect of creation and its symbolic value: like man and all living things, the environment has its natural rhythm which cannot be ignored with degrading it[410]; the land must be given a rest and not abused to the point of barrenness as if it were a disposable commodity[411]; the earth, like life itself, proclaims the glory of God,[412] is good,[413] and is in that regard loved by God himself.[414]

8. Respect for creation cannot coincide with present lifestyle

The lifestyle of hedonism, consumerism, and maximized profit are in direct opposition to the proper valuation of natural resources and ecology,[415] whether we are talking about its consideration as capital, the enrichment provided by its beauty, or its witness to God's glory. Of these, the latter two are particularly non-economic values which market logic cannot in any way account for.[416] In fact, it is difficult to

---

[407] *Rom* 1:20.
[408] *LS,* 233.
[409] St. John of the Cross, *Cántico Espiritual,* XIV, 5.
[410] *SRS,* 26.
[411] *Lev* 25:1-7.
[412] *Dan* 3:56-82.
[413] *Gen* 1:1-31.
[414] *Mt* 6:25-34.
[415] *CV,* 51.
[416] *CA,* 40.

conceive of the environmental problem outside of the context of modern economic errors such as maximized profit and the consumerist mentality.[417] The doctrine of self-interest in particular has no place in a society respectful of the environment,[418] which cannot withstand opportunistic exploitation with no regard to the present or future state of humanity. Concern for the created world is a duty—a possession of God's gifted to the whole human race[419]—and must be considered as linked with the principle of the universal destination of goods. To squander resources and sully the land is not merely to be guilty of individual acts of irresponsibility, but is to directly attack the rights of others:

> "The environment is God's gift to everyone, and in our use of it we have a responsibility towards the poor, towards future generations and towards humanity as a whole...Our duties towards the environment are linked to our duties towards the human person, considered in himself and in relation to others. It would be wrong to uphold one set of duties while trampling on the other."[420]

9. Human ecology

The parallel between our attitude toward nature and that which we display toward ourselves as persons has been spoken of by the popes as the *human ecology*:

> "The deterioration of nature is... closely connected to the culture that shapes human coexistence: when 'human ecology' is respected within society, environmental ecology also benefits."[421]

In employing this phrase, they mean to illustrate that the processes and thriving of humanity are fostered by respect for the processes and

---

[417] *CA*, 37.
[418] *SRS*, 34.
[419] *Lev* 25:23.
[420] *CV*, 48, 51.
[421] Benedict XVI, *General Audience*, August 26, 2009.

thriving of nature. If you care little for the one, you will unintentionally despise the other:

> "If there is a lack of respect for the right to life and to a natural death, if human conception, gestation and birth are made artificial, if human embryos are sacrificed to research, the conscience of society ends up losing the concept of human ecology and, along with it, that of environmental ecology. It is contradictory to insist that future generations respect the natural environment when our educational systems and laws do not help them to respect themselves. The book of nature is one and indivisible: it takes in not only the environment but also life, sexuality, marriage, the family, social relations: in a word, integral human development."[422]

To teach children moral norms such as natural family planning, and then show utter disregard for the overarching world which inform these norms, is to undermine the teachings themselves by dividing a conclusion from its logical demonstration. How could the dictates of natural law be taken seriously when those who preach them take no care for nature itself?

10. Population control is not the answer

For society to close itself to human life would not be a legitimate means of opening itself to other forms of life on this planet. The one need not suffer at the expense of the other, but they must both be respected in their proper order. Those who propose mandated birth control or abortion as the proper means of solving the environmental crisis are taking the easy way out and degrading human life in the process.[423] Such a solution attempts to fix the problem without discipline and without having to change our lifestyle of excess. It amounts to denial of the real causes, which lie elsewhere: "To blame population growth instead of extreme and selective consumerism on the part of some, is one way of refusing to face the issues."[424]

---

[422] *CA*, 37.
[423] *LS*, 117; 120.

11. Disregard for nature will provoke a response

It is not uncommon to dismiss all these warning with a wave of the hand, and trust instead in man's ingenuity, believing that he will continue to adapt, develop, and "conquer" whatever problems may arise in the future. Such is the implicit faith in the ideology of "necessary progress," which really amounts to a faith in man and a denial of limits. But St. John Paul II offers a warning:

> "Instead of carrying out his role as a co-operator with God in the work of creation, man sets himself up in place of God and thus ends up provoking a rebellion on the part of nature, which is more tyrannized than governed by him."[425]

And he is affirmed by Benedict XVI:

> "The relationship between individuals or communities and the environment ultimately stems from their relationship with God. When 'man turns his back on the Creator's plan, he provokes a disorder which has inevitable repercussions on the rest of the created order."[426]

---

[424] *LS*, 50.

[425] Ibid.

[426] Benedict XVI, *Letter to the Ecumenical Patriarch of Constantinople on the Occasion of the Seventh Symposium of the Religion, Science and the Environment Movement*, September 1, 2007.

Section VIII. War

The Church teaches that "insofar as men are sinful, the threat of war hangs over them, and hang over them it will until the return of Christ."[427]

Yet because of this truth we must never forget that there are "strict conditions for legitimate defense by military force."[428] These conditions, known as *just war doctrine*, provide rulers and ruled with a coherent means for evaluating the validity of military action in any conflict. Such a means is vital for any government, particularly in democracies, because in the absence of objective criteria for determining military action, passion and opportunity tend to rule supreme. Ignorance of these principles leads inevitably to atrocities, and the United States, having little regard for Catholic philosophy, is no exception. It violated just war doctrine to great extremes during the Civil War, World War I, and World War II, for example the firebombing of Dresden and the atomic bombings of Hiroshima and Nagasaki. On other points, however, we will see that the United States has behaved with exceptional nobility, and in perfect adherents with certain elements of the doctrine—for example in the treatment of prisoners and many non-combatants. Unfortunately, however, since the doctrine is not acknowledged openly, it is only followed haphazardly and unconsciously, and we have no way of knowing whether this will change tomorrow.

The principles are summarized in the *Catechism*, paragraph 2302-2317, although their formation goes back to St. Augustine (354-430AD) and continued to be affirmed and developed through St. Thomas Aquinas (1225-1274AD) and later theologians as occasion has arisen. This subject is of particular importance for our contemporaries because of the challenge of terrorism, which has fueled new debates and new questions regarding the nature of legitimate defense. So often we run up against the assumption that our problems, because they are new, cannot be addressed by traditional principles, but that is the beauty of *principles.*

---

[427] *GS*, 78.
[428] *CCC*, 2309.

that they are universal, applicable in any age, and need only to be re-applied according to changing circumstances. We will find that this is precisely the case with just war doctrine and the war on terror.

1. Jus ad bellum, or "the right to go to war"

First we must make a distinction between the decision to go to war and the proper behavior during war. This is because the state of war differs from the state of peace, and it would be inappropriate to judge each action *in the midst of war* as we would judge an action in times of peace. The principles guiding the decision to go to war fall under a heading known as *jus ad bellum* or "the right to go to war."

a. Righteous Anger vs. Wrath

Anger is a legitimate response to injustice, just as the Lord expressed anger in the Temple toward the money-changers, going so far as to strike them with whips, driving them from the place. We would call this righteous anger, but before we do so we need understand why it is *righteous* anger expressed through righteous action, and not wrath expressed through illicit violence.

First, anger is a passion with which we react to evil and desire the restoration of justice. As a passion, anger is neither moral or immoral in itself, but becomes one or the other depending on whether or not it is properly ordered and felt in the appropriate degree. If anger is at the wrong object or to a greater or lesser degree than appropriate, then it becomes a vice. We must emphasize here that the *lack of anger* at injustice is an evil of "defect," just as excessive anger is an evil of "excess." Returning to the example of Christ in the Temple, we can say that if a man in that situation had gone any further than Christ, or had neglected to do anything at all, he would have fallen into one or the other evils. Anger should spur us to restore a balance that has been lost—the balance of justice.

Although we have mentioned primarily anger as a passion, we should always connect this with its expression through action: both are separate, as internal and external phenomena, and a man may be right in one but wrong in the other. He may feel an appropriate degree of anger and at the correct object, but his actions may be clumsy or excessive in their effect.

In any consideration of military action we must analyze our passions and ensure that we are not driven by a passion that is excessive, debilitated by one that is deficient, and that our anger is directed toward the proper object.

b. Strict conditions

We may list here the conditions, as presented in the *Catechism*, for the legitimate use of military force (2309):

- the damage inflicted by the aggressor on the nation or community of nations must be lasting, grave, and certain;

- all other means of putting an end to it must have been shown to be impractical or ineffective;

- there must be serious prospects of success;

- the use of arms must not produce evils and disorders graver than the evil to be eliminated. The power of modern means of destruction weighs very heavily in evaluating this condition

We will proceed through each of these with brief comment, but for the moment it is necessary to take notice of the words preceding this list in the *Catechism*, "At one and the same time," are of great import to our reasoning. The conditions set forth are not to be used in an "either...or" process of reasoning. One, or even two, of the conditions may be met, but this does not justify military force. *All* conditions must be met, or we must exclude military force as a just course of action.

c. Lasting, grave, and certain

This first condition is the most demanding: it places before us three elements which must *all* be met in order to justify military force. If the threat is grave but not certain, or certain but not grave, or certain and grave but not lasting, then war is not justified. For this reason, it is this first condition which is most often ignored, with nations going to war or, in the case of the United States forcing Japan to open itself to trade with the West, threatening war, over nothing but economic advantage; or, in the case of the war in Iraq, wars are entered on hearsay and loose hypothesis.

Furthermore, even if this condition—the most stringent—is met, we can then proceed to the remaining conditions, which must also be met. *All* of these conditions must be met *each and every* time.

d. All other means exhausted

There is a time to kill, says King Solomon.[429] But when is this time, and how do we know it has arrived? We are often reminded that war is always the "last resort." This is true, of course, but we must be careful not to be misled by it. It creates the image of a timeline with war at the far end, and on which all other points must be crossed before war is reached and becomes legitimate. While this principle seems intuitive, we must keep in mind that prudence does not require that every alternative actually be attempted before military action takes place; in some cases, if it becomes undeniably clear that postponed military action would be disastrous, then the possibility of certain alternatives can be considered dangerous and futile. Thus, it is important that all the possible points on the timeline be tried before war, but in the event that they are not possible, they may be passed over. Perhaps, then, a better way to say this is that war is not permissible so long as any other non-violent option is actually possible. If no other alternative is possible, then it can be considered an exhausted possibility even if it has not been attempted.

e. Prospects of success

It is not possible to be certain of success in war, regardless of superiority of technology or numbers, as the United States learned in Vietnam. Thus, we see that the third condition—"serious prospects of success"—is not so demanding as the first condition. Regarding the threat, we must be absolutely certain; regarding our success, we need only be reassured

---

[429] *Eccl* 3:3.

that there is a substantial possibility. If the endeavor is futile, then it is unjust to sacrifice lives in its pursuit.

f. Must not produce greater evils

Here we are concerned with the consequences of war insofar as they are possible to foresee. On this point we must remember St. John Paul II's dictum, that unintended consequences of any action will often outnumber the intended, because a rational calculation of all effects is impossible.[430] But whatever consequences we are able to calculate must be seriously weighed and must not constitute an evil greater than the original.

g. Competent authority

Finally, we must ask who makes the final decision to go to war? Which is to ask who is responsible for producing a judgment based on these criteria:

> "The evaluation of these conditions for moral legitimacy belongs to the prudential judgment of those who have responsibility for the common good."[431]

The public authority, then, because it is responsible for the national defense is also responsible for judging when and how to employ military force for the sake of that defense. Such a condition is difficult to accept under the aegis of democracy because the citizens have come to see themselves as the actual governors, rather than the electors of their governors which then govern on the basis of information and perspective that the electors cannot have. This confusion results in a mentality through which the average voter believes he has, or should have, the proper information before him necessary to pronounce on every question of military intervention, and in addition should have his pronouncements put into effect. Unfortunately, the attempt to base military action on public opinion in this way results almost each and

---

[430] *VS*, 77.
[431] *CCC*, 2309.

every time in a total disregard for each condition of just war. That is not to say that governments are more likely to take just war into account, but it is possible for them to do so should they set themselves to the task; it is not possible for the uninformed citizen to do so, whether he wants to or not.

2. Jus in bello, or "right conduct in war"

Once a decision has been made and the state of war is entered, we must change our perspective, for to treat every decision in the midst of war as if it were being made in the midst of peace would be inappropriate and, if we were indeed justified in our decision to enter the conflict, unnecessary. We find in the state of war, then, a new set of conditions, and these fall under the heading of *jus in bello*, or "right conduct in war."

Perhaps the most important point made by the Church is that the moral law remains in effect during war, just as it does any other time. The dictum, "all is fair in love and war," which men are so quick to adopt in order to excuse any sort of action, must be rejected out of hand.[432]

a. Non-combatants

In sections 2313 and 2314 the *Catechism* emphasizes the point that non-combatants are never to be targeted during war—not for any reason or under any circumstances. To treat prisoners inhumanely or target civilian populations is a "crime against God and man." The United States has been on both sides of this question, famous for its humane treatment of prisoners and civilians in certain conflicts, yet infamous for directly targeting entire populations at others. This principle has become more significant as technology has advanced, whether we are speaking of nuclear weapons or biological/chemical warfare, because it is usually the richer or more developed nations who have these and who are therefore susceptible to the temptation to employ them.

---

[432] *CCC*, 2312.

b. The law of double-effect

Perfection is not demanded by the Church. Catholic theology allows for the possibility that an act has good and evil consequences, and in this it has acknowledged the law of double-effect. To use one of Aquinas's examples, it is not licit to wish to kill a man, but one may employ lethal force in one's own defense. The act has the double effect, but it was permissible because, although the evil was foreseen, it was for the sake of the immediate good—self-preservation—that the act was actually carried out. The death of the attacker was an unwilled, even if foreseeable, consequence of the justified response of the victim.

To apply this to war, it is often unavoidable that collateral damage will occur in a conflict; yet the collateral damage can never be the direct intention of the attacker. To mention again the bombings of Dresden, Hiroshima, and Nagasaki, civilization populations were directly targeted as a means of pressuring their government's to submit. Because the targeting of civilians was the *direct* intention of the attacks, it would not fall under the law of double-effect and was an offense to just war doctrine.

3. Disarmament

Because all nations are obligated to work toward peace, and because the possession of weapons is justified only insofar as the maintenance of peace is justified, then it seems that arms themselves, their purchase and sale, and the quantity produced and maintained by a nation, as objects of concern for the Social Doctrine of the Church. For this reason, arms cannot be treated like a simple category of goods to be bought and sold on the international or domestic market.[433]

The Church does not agree with the prevalent notion that stockpiling arms, particularly nuclear arms, is an effective or necessary means of achieving peace: "The accumulation of arms strikes many as a paradoxically suitable way of deterring potential adversaries from war. They see it as the most effective means of ensuring peace among

---

[433] *CSDC,* 508.

nations. This method of deterrence gives rise to strong moral reservations. The arms race does not ensure peace. Far from eliminating the causes of war, it risks aggravating them."[434] Rather, a policy of non-proliferation combined with widespread reduction in nuclear arms, and arms that strike indiscriminately (for example, landmines), is the path recommended by the Magisterium.

4. Terrorism

The rise of terrorist activity on a global scale has made the maintenance of just military a difficult one indeed, for not only are terrorist organizations not often governmental organizations, but they also claim to be acting on behalf of the religious beliefs of large groups. Nonetheless, terrorism has been addressed directly and in no uncertain terms by the Magisterium, summarized in paragraphs 513-515 of the *Compendium*, in addition to forming a main point of comment in various *World Peace Day* addresses which the popes are accustomed to delivering.

First, because terrorist groups have claimed religious, rather than ideological, motivations, terrorism has fueled the long-standing myth that religion itself is an inherently violent phenomenon. This myth has been fashionable in the West for several centuries, and serves to affirm the prejudices of secular regimes, reinforcing the notion that the more "contained" and excluded are religions from the public sphere, particularly politics, the better off the world will be. The popes are careful to reject this notion in particular, saying that "hatred, fanaticism and terrorism profane the name of God and disfigure the true image of man."[435] "It is a profanation and a blasphemy to declare oneself a terrorist in God's name."[436]

Moreover, the Church has attempted to separate violence done *in the name of religion* from the religion itself, reminding the world that

---

[434] *CCC*, 2315.
[435] St. John Paul II, *Address to Representatives from the World of Culture, Art and Science* (24 September 2001), 5.
[436] *CSDC*, 515.

criminal responsibility is always *personal*, and it is a minority group of individuals who commit these atrocities.[437]

The problem itself has also been viewed by the Church as a call to more than just military action and manhunts. It has been said that this problem calls also for understanding and reflection:

> "[T]he fight against terrorism cannot be limited solely to repressive and punitive operations. It is essential that the use of force, even when necessary, be accompanied by a courageous and lucid analysis of the reasons behind terrorist attacks. The fight against terrorism must be conducted also on the political and educational levels...by eliminating the underlying causes of situations of injustice which frequently drive people to more desperate and violent acts..."[438]

For many people it is difficult to accept that the idea atrocities committed by terrorists may be in some degree caused by the actions of the groups they attack; to merely suggest such a thing smacks of injustice, and seems to suggest that we are exonerating the men who have brutalized our civilian populations. But this is not the case: the Church does not attempt to remove blame from the terrorists, but wishes us to view every chain of events with open eyes. It is easy to cry "They hate our freedoms," and then leave things at that, but such slogans are usually childish attempts to avoid having to search out real causes for concrete events, which are always much more complicated and occasionally unpleasant for us to grapple with.

Lastly, the popes call men to avoid the temptation which has grown up with terrorism, and which represents in fact one of terrorism's greatest victories, which is the urge to discard traditional norms and procedures, and to ignore respect due to human life on the grounds that the terrorists have done so themselves. Far from being led down this road of self-degradation and anarchy, the Church teaches that such situations

---

[437] *CSDC*, 514.
[438] St. John Paul II, *Message for the 2004 World Day of Peace*, 8.

demand new cooperation among nations, and not a rejection but a re-affirmation of the value of human life, international norms, and cooperative procedures in order to help fight this plague.[439]

St. John Paul II summarizes the evil, saying: "Those who kill by acts of terrorism actually despair of humanity, of life, of the future. In their view, everything is to be hated and destroyed."[440]

And Benedict XVI points to the path necessary to solve this problem, which is not the abandoning of law and human dignity, adopting the methods of terror, torture, and injustice ourselves, but rather it calls for a greater proclamation of the Christian message than ever before:

> "In view of the risks which humanity is facing in our time, all Catholics in every part of the world have a duty to proclaim and embody ever more fully the "Gospel of Peace", and to show that acknowledgment of the full truth of God is the first, indispensable condition for consolidating the truth of peace."[441]

And a final warning from one of the Church's most recent canonized saints, which is that there can be,

> "*No peace without justice, no justice without forgiveness.* I shall not tire of repeating this warning to those who, for one reason or another, nourish feelings of hatred, a desire for revenge or the will to destroy."[442]

---

[439] Benedict XVI, *Message for the 2007 World Day of Peace*, 14; St. John Paul II, *Message for the 2004 World Day of Peace*, 8.

[440] St. John Paul II, *Message for the 2002 World Day of Peace*, 6.

[441] Benedict XVI, *Message for the 2006 World Day of Peace*, 11.

[442] John Paul II, *Message for the 2001 World Day of Peace*, 15.

Printed in Great Britain
by Amazon